SECRETS
OF THE
SCREEN TRADE
FROM CONCEPT TO SALE

ALLEN B. URY

 lone eagle

Secrets of the Screen Trade
From Concept to Sale
Copyright © 2005 Fade In Publishing Group, Inc.

LONE EAGLE PUBLISHING COMPANY
5055 Wilshire Blvd.
Los Angeles, CA 90036
Phone 800.815.0503
www.hcdonline.com

Printed in the United States of America
10 9 8 7 6 5 4 3 2 1

Cover design by Lindsay Albert
Book design by Carla Green

Library of Congress Cataloging-in-Publication Data

Ury, Allen B.
Secrets of the screen trade / by Allen B. Ury.
        p. cm.
      ISBN 1-58065-060-0
      1. Motion picture authorship. 2. Motion picture authorship—Marketing. I. Title.

      PN1996.U78 2004
      808.2'3—dc22   2004057622

Books may be purchased in bulk at special discounts for promotional or educational purposes. Special editions can be created to specifications. Inquiries for sales and distribution, textbook adoption, foreign language translation, editorial, and rights and permissions inquiries should be addressed to: Jeff Black, Lone Eagle Publishing, 5055 Wilshire Blvd., Los Angeles, CA 90036 or send e-mail to info@loneeagle.com.

Distributed to the trade by National Book Network, 800-462-6420.

Lone Eagle Publishing Company™ is a registered trademark.

CONTENTS

STORYTELLING

MECHANICS

THE SALE

ACKNOWLEDGEMENTS

Naturally, books — like life — are not born in a vacuum. Many people must be acknowledged for helping me write the articles that appear in this book, as well as for adding to my still-growing understanding of the screenwriting craft and the Byzantine world that is Hollywood.

Thanks must go to my editor and the publisher of *Fade In* magazine, Audrey Kelly, without whom this book simply would not exist. The woman's energy, perseverance, and demand for excellence never cease to amaze me.

I would also like to acknowledge all of the wonderful, talented, and generous working writers I've interviewed over the years, including Buck Henry, Larry Gelbart, Michael Givens, Robert Towne, Lowell Ganz & Babaloo Mandel, and Scott Alexander & Larry Karaszewski. Also the various producers and studio executives I've had the pleasure of working with over the years, including Bruce A. Block, Joe Wizan, Peter Rosten, Charles Hirschhorn, Jim Weeda, Michael Peyser, and Jag Mundhra.

Finally, no amount of gratitude is sufficient to thank my wife — my soulmate and my bridge back to reality — Rene. Also to our son, Robert, for only making fun of me in private.

FOREWORD

Back in the mid-1980s, *Esquire* magazine featured a memorable cover photo of a chimpanzee energetically pecking at a typewriter. The accompanying headline inquired, perhaps not facetiously, "Is *Everyone* in America Writing a Screenplay?"

During those halcyon days of the Reagan Administration, it did seem as if Hollywood's allure — while always powerful — had suddenly taken on a whole new and decidedly more profound dimension. Even as The Great Communicator was going eyeball-to-eyeball with the Evil Empire, weekly box office grosses — once the limited purview of industry trade magazines — were suddenly popping up in daily newspapers from Portland to Peoria. Syndicated entertainment news shows like *Entertainment Tonight* were making Hollywood dish a dinnertime staple. Periodicals like *Premiere* and *Entertainment Weekly* were elevating "movie fan magazine" from the realm of supermarket tabloid to that of airport newsstand legitimacy.

With everyone from cab drivers to cardiologists suddenly an "expert" on movie-making, it's no wonder that everyone wanted in on the action. However, few folks possessed the superior physical attributes or the god-given talent needed to be movie stars, nor did they have the experience, technical know-how, or bankable track records required to direct.

So what was left?

Screenwriting!

Indeed, screenwriting appeared to be the easiest way for Joe Everyman (and Jane Everywoman) to buy a ticket in the La-La Land Lotto. Instead of taking years of acting lessons or interning for bup-

kis on some shoestring straight-to-video stinker, all you really needed to go straight to the A-List was a Smith-Corona, 120 pages of
white twenty-pound bond paper, and a rudimentary mastery of high
school-level English. You could be fat, bald, cross-eyed, and bow-
legged and *still* bag a quick 300 grand for your story about an alco-
holic cop who gets partnered with a talking llama to bust a gang of
South American drug lords. Heck, you didn't even need to be in
Southern California to *write.*

Articles in mainstream publications like *The Wall Street Journal*
profiling young writers who were making mid-six-figure incomes
writing screenplays that didn't even get *produced* only added high-
octane gasoline to the already raging inferno that was our shared
dream of a "Screenplay by" credit. (In the final episode of ABC-TV's
long running sitcom, *Happy Days*, aired in May 1984, even squeaky-
clean Richie Cunningham, played by Ron Howard, ran off to Los
Angeles to be a screenwriter. Gee, what ever happened to *him*?)

America's publishing industry was more than happy to accom-
modate the ranks of Robert Towne/William Goldman wannabes by
releasing what quickly became a small flood of "how-to" books
revealing the arcane secrets of the once-private world of the
Hollywood screenwriter. The principal focus of these books was
"structure," a concept that could be summarized in three words:
Beginning, Middle, and End. The premise of these books — and the
many more that followed — was that if certain events happened at
certain times relative to a screenplay's total page count — *voila!* —
you had a movie.

So persuasive were these tomes that the terms they coined —
"plot point," "inciting incident," "reversal," "character arc," etc. —
have since become part of the Hollywood lexicon. Everyone in the
industry — from the just-hired "D-girl" to the most powerful mogul
— is by now intimately familiar with "The Three-Act Paradigm"
and knows its "rules" — excuse me, "guidelines" — the way the
Pope knows the King James Bible.

Like so many other children of the '70s, I, too, was beckoned
westward by Hollywood's siren song. Armed with a Radio-TV-Film
Degree from the University of Wisconsin-Madison and enough paid
experience in advertising and public relations to earn a living "in the
meantime," I landed on the West Coast in 1983 and immediately
began plying my wares to whomever would listen. Landing an agent
almost immediately on the strength of a spec comedy titled

Comrades, Inc. (a Cold War-era farce about con men who rent them-selves out as recyclable "Communist rebels" to corrupt South American despots eager to get money from the CIA), I began selling spec scripts and pitches to the likes of Walt Disney Studios, New Line Cinema, Fries Entertainment, producer Joe Wizan, and others. I joined the Writers Guild of America-West in 1988, wrote some straight-to-video thrillers, did some syndicated TV work and, dur-ing this same period, wrote and published nearly twenty juvenile horror novels (a story in itself).

As my fortunes rose and fell, I also freelanced as a "reader" for Interscope Communications and Cinema Line Films, where I got the opportunity to read and evaluate scores of "hot-off-the-presses" screenplays from virtually every writer working at the time.

It was also in the early 1990s that, through my agent, I was intro-duced to Audrey Kelly, an exceedingly bright and savvy young woman who was, at the time, just forming a screenwriters support group called "The Writers Network." She was putting together a stable of "analysts" who could help member writers — most of them unproduced — whip their spec scripts into marketable shape. TWN would then help set these scripts up with one of the network of agents at major talent agencies with whom Audrey already had extensive contacts.

Based on the strength of my produced credits and reader work, I was offered an analyst position. The gig sounded like an interest-ing one, and I've been with Audrey ever since. During the past decade, I have analyzed and written extensive reports for well over 500 screenplays, and have read at least 2,000 more as a judge in the annual screenwriting contests sponsored by The Writers Network and the entertainment magazine *Fade In*.

I've also been lucky enough to be a staff writer for *Fade In*, con-ducting interviews with some of this business' legendary screenwrit-ers, including Robert Towne (*Chinatown*), Buck Henry (*The Graduate*), Lowell Ganz & Babaloo Mandel (*City Slickers*), and Scott Alexander & Larry Karaszewski (*The People vs. Larry Flynt*).

This wide range of experience writing scripts, reading scripts, evaluating scripts, and interviewing other writers led me to serious-ly reconsider all I had encountered in more than a dozen screenwrit-ing books I'd read over the past two decades. My conclusions:
1) Most of them were right;
2) What they offered wasn't enough.

Just as Copernicus' model of a sun-centered universe explained some — but not all — of our celestial observations, so did the classic theories of the Three Act Paradigm of Character Arc help writers tackle some — but not all — of the challenges that face us every time we face that blank computer screen. Why, for example, if the classic first act "Plot Point" isn't supposed to occur until page 30, do scripts that follow this formula seem to drag initially? If jeopardy was supposed to escalate during Act Two, why do movies like *Home Alone* and, more recently, *About Schmidt*, succeed with both critics and audiences — despite having virtually no meaningful action in their middle hours? And why, despite following formula to a "T," do so many writers have trouble writing action films and thrillers that carry any degree of emotional resonance?

Helping members of The Writers Network address these and other practical issues led to me developing my own set of rules and/or guidelines that I then, in classic scientific fashion, tested rigorously against every screenplay I read and every motion picture I saw. Those theories that held up I committed to paper in the form of "how-do" articles published in *Fade In* magazine, a series that eventually became known as "Master Class" (Editor Audrey Kelly's title, not mine). Over the years, these articles covered the gamut from developing a marketable premise to creating viable villains to writing effective set-pieces to writing to please professional readers.

Now, Audrey has collected my "greatest hits" in this single volume. All of the articles assume that you, the reader, already have a working knowledge of screenwriting, that you've studied the form, and are even familiar — perhaps intimately so — with the "how-to" books and screenwriting "gurus" who have come before me. Good. That's a start. Now, to paraphrase Sir Issac Newton, it's time to "stand on the shoulders of giants" and look beyond the old horizon to find — we hope — new and better ways to address those problems that have vexed every dramatist from Sophocles to Charlie Kaufman.

Take a seat. Open your notebooks.

Master Class is in session.

STORYTELLING

BREAKTHROUGH GENRES
The Stories Hollywood Wants You to Write

When advising unproduced writers on story selection, Hollywood gurus will inevitably tell you, "Write from the heart," or, "Write the story *you* want to write." While passion is unquestionably a key element in all good writing — screen or otherwise — writing your "dream screenplay" right out of the box can prove counter-productive, especially if the script you're just dying to write is a lavish musical, a sprawling western, or the next James Bond film.

If you're serious about being a professional screenwriter, your long-term interests will be far better served if you keep your artistic ambitions temporarily in check and instead write a script in a genre that offers the best chance for an actual sale. As Hollywood can be one of the toughest of industries to enter, new writers are best advised to "follow the path of least resistance" and keep their dream projects tucked away until they have the power and influence necessary to break through the barriers that confront even the most seasoned filmmakers.

If this sounds like an artistic sell-out, be advised that virtually all of Hollywood's top writers and writer-directors launched their careers by writing down-and-dirty genre films to establish their professional credentials. For example, before Andy and Larry Wachowski made *The Matrix*, they wrote and directed a little lesbian crime thriller called *Bound*. Before James Cameron made *Titanic*, he wrote and directed a low-budget sci-fi action piece called *The Terminator*. Long before *Back to the Future*, *Forrest Gump*, *Who Framed Roger Rabbit*, and *Cast Away*, Robert Zemeckis and his co-writer Bob Gale were pumping out low-budget comedies like *I Wanna Hold Your Hand* and *Used Cars*.

When choosing a genre for a spec script, here are some key factors to keep in mind:

Producers and studios are historically averse to taking risks. They therefore gravitate toward genres with large, established audiences (e.g. action, comedy, teen) and avoid those that have proven to be "hard sells" (e.g. musicals, period dramas, westerns).

Producers and studios can mitigate their risks by minimizing their investments. Therefore, a script that is less expensive to produce will be more attractive than one that will cost megabucks to put on the silver screen. Scripts that feature lots of interiors and can be shot close to home (i.e., Los Angeles) will win favor over screenplays with numerous exterior scenes or that require exotic locations (mountains, deserts, foreign countries).

Since nearly two-thirds of a movie's income can now come from video sales/rentals and overseas box office, scripts in genres that have proven appeal in foreign and ancillary markets will score points over those that don't. Although "hot" genres change from week to week depending on what's Number One at the box office, certain genres have historically proven to be writer-friendly, especially for writers without established credits. If you're looking to make your first sale to a studio-affiliated producer or other mainstream buyer, here are the genres in which you should be working:

Thrillers: Tight, clever, high-concept thrillers always have been and will always be great vehicles for new writers. Films like *Phone Booth* and *Identity* may not set box office records, but they tend to be inexpensive to make, do very well in home video, and, most importantly: *They get their writers noticed.* And with A-list casting and directors, "little" thrillers like *Panic Room* can become big films.

Noir: A subgenre of the traditional thriller, the noir (short for film noir) is dark, bleak, often sexually charged, and concerned almost exclusively with human corruption. Usually small and featuring contained violence (if someone is shot or stabbed it's a noir; if there's a car chase, it's an action film), noir features such as the Coen Brothers' *Blood Simple*, Christopher McQuarrie's *The Usual Suspects*, or Christopher Nolan's *Memento* tend to become audience and critical favorites — and frequently earn attention from Academy voters as well.

Horror: During the 1970s and 1980s, dozens of young writers and directors cut their professional teeth on low-budget horror films that teens gobbled up like so many Pac Man dots. Even today, relatively cheap, youth-oriented horror projects like *The Blair Witch Project*, *Final Destination*, and *Scream* continue to draw crowds and make instant celebrities out of their creators. As with thrillers, put an A-List star in the project, and suddenly a little four-character horror piece like *The Sixth Sense* can become a career-maker.

Action Movies: Like thrillers, good action movies always sell. They not only tend to do well at the box office, but their popularity overseas is legend. But be careful. Action tends to be expensive, and for unproduced writers, it's far smarter to write a "contained" action film with psychological overtones (e.g., *The Game*, *Fight Club*) than something you hope will be the next Jerry Bruckheimer opus.

"Small" Sci-Fi: Science-fiction projects that are smart, take place in the present, and require only limited visual and make-up effects are an ideal way for "new" writers to grab the industry's attention. Examples of such "small" sci-fi films include the remake of *The Fly*, as well as *The Terminator* and *Frequency*.

Comedies: Your script can be a romantic comedy, a broad comedy, a teen comedy, an institutional comedy — it doesn't matter. There's only one rule here: If they're laughing, they're buying.

On the flipside, there are a host of genres that tend to be "poison" to unproduced writers. Yes, these kinds of screenplays do get sold — just not by *you*. By definition, these genres represent higher risks to the studios, and therefore require the hiring of established, A-List writers whose involvement allow the executives in charge to plead due diligence if or when the movies flop.

Genres to avoid include:
- Small, character-driven "slice of life" stories*
- Ensemble pieces*
- Space operas
- Animated films
- Musicals
- Sequels and remakes (Unless you own the rights)
- Fantasy/New Age
- Adult romances*
- Adult dramas*
- Historical epics
- Westerns

STORYTELLING

- Whodunits
- Biographies
- Pirate Movies (*Pirates of the Caribbean* notwithstanding)

* These genres may still find favor in the Independent market.

Although these guidelines may seem restrictive to writers with ambitions beyond the thriller/horror/comedy arena, remember that, like the proverbial 1,000-mile journey, all professional careers must begin with a first step. With a script sold, a movie made, and a reputation established, you'll find that your creative options will suddenly increase a dozen-fold. The trick is to make that first sale. And history has shown us a clear path.

Today, *Last Woman on Earth*; tomorrow, *Mystic River.*

STRANGE BREW
Are You Writing a Motion Picture — Or Something Else?

Screenplays can take anywhere from several weeks to several years to write. However many hours your particular script demands from you, it represents a sizable investment of time and energy. It's a chunk of your life you'll never get back.

You must therefore ask yourself some hard, practical questions before you put your first word on paper (or onto your hard drive). Regardless of how wonderful you think your story is, you must first ask yourself, "But is it a *movie*?"

This is a critical question, because not all stories make good motion pictures. Even *great* stories may not warrant feature-film treatment. Some stories simply make better novels. Or short stories. Or stageplays. Or TV movies or miniseries. (That these forms are not equivalent explains why many successful books and plays often become cinematic bombs, and why screenplay novelizations rarely make great literature.)

How can you tell the difference between a movie-friendly story and something else? Ask yourself these basic questions when judging your intended screen treatment:

Is your narrative complex enough to fill two full hours? There are many stories that, while excellent, simply aren't complicated enough to be stretched to feature-film length. Such stories tend to start with an interesting character, have that character face an intriguing problem or situation, then the hero solves his or her problem and the story is over. Such stories often make good short stories, short films, or even TV episodes. However, when stretched to feature-film length, these stories tend to drag and feel "padded" because there just isn't enough going on.

One reason why many TV series don't make good movie adaptations is because their dramatic architectures demand that their conflicts be resolved within twenty-two to fifty minutes. This is particularly true of situation comedies, which tend to lack the kind of narrative complexity, dramatic depth, and character development we expect from feature films.

Conversely, some stories are just too long to be squeezed into the limited feature-film format. Sprawling, complex novels often feel thin and truncated, or like a collection of highlights when pared down to a two- or even three-hour running time. If you have a grand, massive epic in mind, your best shot may be to write it as a novel or, if you have the clout to get it seriously considered, as a TV miniseries. (Note: Unproduced screenwriters don't get to write network TV miniseries. Put the thought out of your mind because it just doesn't happen.)

Does your story contain sufficient conflict? Drama is, by its very nature, the study of forces in opposition and the changes that occur as a result. A piece of writing that emphasizes that conflict — particularly man-vs.-man and man-vs.-nature — has the potential to make effective motion pictures. On the other hand, writing that is primarily focused on mood, emotion, description, or the classic "man against himself" conflict may be best suited for novels or short stories.

Is your story about your character's external or internal life? Movies, by definition, *move*. They're about characters in *physical motion*. A story about a woman who has forty-eight hours to get from New York to Los Angeles to collect a $1 million inheritance — and she's scared to death of airplanes — might make a good movie. On the other hand, a story about a man sitting at a bar reflecting on his crumbling marriage would probably make a much better short story than a film.

In fact, any story that principally involves someone *thinking* is probably *not* feature-film material. A story that principally involves someone *doing* probably *is*. Clue: If your screenplay contains a lot of voice-over, you've probably got a novel, not a movie.

Does your story have physical scope? One thing that film does better than any other medium is take us to multiple, perhaps far-flung locations in the literal wink of an eye. Whereas the novelist or short-story writer may take several sentences, paragraphs, or even pages to properly describe a location, the filmmaker can do it with one well-staged shot. It is therefore incumbent upon the screenwriter to take the fullest advantage of the medium's power by "opening up" his or her story through the use of multiple settings and visually interesting locations.

So, for example, if your story is about two people having a brilliant, entertaining discussion around a dinner table, it's probably a stageplay (and that's exactly what 1981's *My Dinner with Andre* was — a filmed stageplay). On the other hand, if your story is about two people having a brilliant, entertaining discussion while they fight their way through the Ardennes Forest during World War II's Battle of the Bulge, you may have yourself a movie.

Note that movies don't need $100 million budgets to have scope. Even simple interior-based dramas and romantic comedies can still look like movies if they employ multiple settings and shift regularly between interior and exterior locations.

Does your story contain extreme elements of foul language, sex, and/or violence? For the first two-thirds of the 20th century, all motion pictures were designed for general audiences. Although the subject matter of individual films necessarily appealed to specific audiences, no major Hollywood movie produced under the Hays Office's Production Code contained verbal or visual material which the vast majority of Americans would find "objectionable." This all changed in the mid-1960s with the introduction of G, PG, R, and X ratings (and later, PG-13 and NC-17). With this new system, filmmakers were given far wider latitude in terms of their treatment of language, sex, and violence — and they have taken full advantage of it. Today, more than half of all movies produced by the major studios are rated R. Add PG-13 films to the mix and you account for more than 80 percent of Hollywood's annual output.

So what's happened to clean, wholesome family films? Films about relationships? Issue-oriented dramas?

They've all gone to television.

Although the output of made-for-TV movies has dropped significantly from its height in the late 1970s and early 1980s, small, intimate films that lack a healthy sex-and-violence quotient are still invariably regarded as potential MOWs (Movies of the Week). The only way to overcome this stigma is to either inject some exploitative elements (one or two well-placed "fucks" will usually suffice) or attach an A-list star. No doubt 1999's *Music of the Heart* would have been a Hallmark Hall of Fame special if Meryl Streep hadn't been its lead. Otherwise, be ready to neatly divide your story into seven acts, leaving plenty of time for commercial breaks.

There is always a market for a good story well told. However, knowing what market best suits the story you wish to tell is your first step toward professional success. Just as Tiger Woods doesn't try to play basketball and the Backstreet Boys don't try to sing opera, don't try to write a feature film if what your story really wants to be is a stageplay, a novel, a short story, or a television MOW.

THE IMPORTANCE OF THEME
What Is This Movie About?

Your screenplay has all the elements necessary for success. It has a smart, tricky plot. Your characters are sharp, original, and multi-dimensional; there's action aplenty and your dialogue crackles like a campfire.

So why hasn't it sold? The answer may go far deeper than such obvious considerations as story, character, structure, pacing, or format. In fact, it may all boil down to the reason you decided to write this particular screenplay in the first place. We're talking about one of the most elusive, yet critical elements in any dramatic story — its theme.

What exactly is theme? The American Heritage *Dictionary of the English Language* defines it as "a topic of discourse or discussion...an implicit or recurrent idea." As that relates to a screenplay, it means: "What is this movie about?" Not, "What happens?" or, "What's the problem?" but: *"What's the point?"*

Most themes can be expressed in shorthand terms. They are elemental issues around which most dramatic stories revolve. Some "classic" themes include: revenge, fate, love, honor, ambition, family, redemption, good vs. evil, and coming of age. Every dramatic story, from the epic poems of Homer to the latest $100 million action flick, uses as its foundation a fundamentally simple idea, from which the author then supplies his or her personal spin.

Here's how some famous movies might boil down under the most basic of definition of theme:

> *Casablanca* — Redemption
> *The Lord of the Rings Trilogy* — Heroism
> *Forrest Gump* — Fate
> *Star Wars* — Good vs. Evil/Coming of Age
> *Citizen Kane* — Corruption
> *Seabiscuit* — Perseverance
> *The Godfather* — Family

Recognizing the core thematic element in any movie, including your own, is only the first step in forming a fully realized theme. Next, you have to express — if only for yourself — your opinion on that issue. That opinion is what ultimately forms the dramatic structure of the story.

It's been said that a good theme is a statement for which a strong argument can be made, either pro or con. For example, the theme of 1995's Best Picture Academy Award-winner, *Braveheart*, could be said to be, "Freedom is worth any price, including one's own life," or, as an earlier sage so aptly put it, "I'd rather die on my feet than live on my knees." What makes this a good theme is that it's just as possible to argue that, "I'd rather live on my knees than die on my feet." In the course of *Braveheart*, William Wallace personifies the first (heroic) argument, whereas most of the Scottish noblemen represent the opposing view, choosing to acquiesce to the brutal English rather put their own lives and property at risk.

Virtually all other successful movies also take a stand concerning their thematic ideas, and then present us with either an antagonist or a supporting character who personifies the opposing point of view. The struggle to prove which argument is stronger forms the basis of the dramatic story.

For example, in 1993's *Schindler's List*, the creator's theme is expressed explicitly in the Talmudic quotation, "He who saves one life saves the world." Another way to say this might be, "It is far better to do even a little good than none at all." Over the course of the story, Oskar Schindler struggles to be as avaricious as he can, yet a core of goodness finally compels him to risk his own life and fortune to save a handful of others. Although only a few people survive due to his efforts, while millions of others die, the results are enough to have him revered as a modern-day saint. In comparison, the brutal German officer, Amon Goeth, responds only to his own selfish, mercenary instincts — resulting in his own ignominious death.

On a lighter note, 1994's Best Picture winner, *Forrest Gump*, again had an explicit theme expressed by the oft-quoted line, "Life is like a box of chocolates — you never know what you're going to get." In other words, life is a series of unpredictable and unexpected events. The protagonist, Forrest Gump, accepts this as an axiom and succeeds beyond anyone's wildest dreams by allowing himself to be swept along by the winds of fate. In comparison, Forrest's commanding officer, Lt. Dan, comes to the game intent on fulfilling what he thinks is his "destiny" — in his case, dying gloriously in battle. When this doesn't come to pass, his life collapses. Ultimately, he learns to "go with the flow" just like Forrest always has, and finds redemption.

As stated earlier, a good dramatic theme is a statement for which a strong argument can be made either pro or con. For this reason, some ideas are so vapid that they make poor dramatic themes. For example, it's easy to argue that "Murder is bad," but very difficult to argue that "Murder is good."

This is one reason why disease or disability usually makes for poor drama. "Cancer is a bad thing" is self evident. So is "Smoking is harmful," "Being drunk is dangerous," or "Losing your legs is not recommended." Who's going to take the opposing point of view seriously?

To help yourself write the best possible screenplay, here are some steps you can take in the area of dramatic theme:

Know what your movie is about. Actually write your theme out in a single line. If you can't do this before you actually start writing your script, be sure you're able to do so by the time you attack your second draft. Theme defines story.

Put your theme in a visible place. Some writers actually tape them to their computer monitor screens. Whenever your story begins to drift or lose focus, you can always refer back to your central idea.

Be sure that your protagonist expresses the "pro" side of your thematic argument, whether that argument is positive ("Good is stronger than Evil") or negative ("Evil is stronger than Good"). Conversely, make sure that at least one of your other characters — usually the antagonist — personifies the "con" side of the debate. Stories work best when the "con" side is just as strong as the "pro" side — or even stronger.

If possible, find an artful way to explicitly express your theme within the body of your movie. This can come in the form of an original catchphrase, a famous quote, or even an applicable joke. (Woody Allen uses several classic Borscht Belt jokes to express the romantic themes of his 1977 Best Picture winner, *Annie Hall*.)

When it comes to selling your talent, mastering the idea of theme can help you enormously as a writer — even if you haven't written a thing. Many verbal pitches are sold not on the basis of their stories ("Well, this happens, then this happens, then this happens...") but on their themes ("This is story about how one person makes a difference...").

Before you type "FADE IN:", before you write your synopsis, before you even come up with a title, be able to answer the question, "What is this movie about?" Once you've answered that, you're already well along the path to success.

MUDDY WATERS
Why Complex Themes Make for Compelling Movies

All successful writers know the value and importance of a good theme. Theme provides narrative direction. Theme dictates structure. Theme answers the key question, "What is this movie about?" And audiences, consciously or not, know the difference between a story that intelligently explores a compelling question and one that is merely a patchwork of related scenes — and respond accordingly.

But unlike people, all themes are not created equal. Some stories contain simple themes: good vs. evil, honesty is the best policy, love conquers all, etc. Such stories tend to deal with one- or two-dimensional characters, have clearly defined protagonists and antagonists, and develop along familiar, predictable paths. They exist, in essence, to support or reinforce established social mores. They're "feel good" pieces that essentially teach us what we already know and tell us what we want to hear.

Other stories explore themes that are more complex. Such stories either turn a familiar bromide on its ear, for example: honesty *isn't* always the best policy, love *doesn't* always conquer all, etc., or they pit two equally valid values against each other, e.g.: love vs. family, family vs. country, law vs. justice, etc.

Commercially speaking, there's a lot to be said for simple themes. Simple themes are easily accessible and digested by mass audiences. People like simple themes precisely because they're not challenging and therefore make them feel comfortable. Of the Top Ten grossing films of all time (worldwide), all were built from simple themes, mostly good vs. evil. (Only the Number One film, 1997's

Titanic, can be said to also employ complex themes, thanks to Writer-Director James Cameron's quasi-Marxist class-conscious approach to the historic disaster.)

However, to get noticed by industry readers, producers and, yes, even cold-hearted studio executives, it often pays to forego the obvious, one-dimensional, simple theme commercial approach to storytelling and choose to explore a theme that is more complex than a cliché like *be yourself*.

This advice may seem paradoxical in an industry that unabashedly worships monetary success beyond all else. However, because simple themes are so easy to dramatize, constructing a screenplay around such a no-brainer does little to illuminate individual creativity or talent. By choosing a theme that is difficult and complex — and then executing your script in a smart, effective manner — you can demonstrate not only that you understand the craft of screenwriting, but that you have a unique voice as well. And if there's one thing that jaded readers, producers, agents, and studio execs always respond to, it's a "unique voice." (Note that "respond to" does not mean the same thing as "buy." Industry folks will often become extremely passionate about a script they feel is wonderfully written yet believe doesn't have a chance in hell of actually selling. The good news is that, if the writers of such "uncommercial" scripts acquire enough fans and continue to deliver superior work, they tend to eventually not only find paying gigs, but become industry darlings as well. Singular writers and writer/directors such as Charlie Kaufman, Wes Anderson, and Neil LaBute all fall into this rarified category.)

So what kind of theme qualifies as "complex" — and how can you translate that theme into a dramatically — or comedically — effective screenplay? Here are some guidelines:

Complex themes usually begin with a question rather than a statement. For example, the *Harry Potter* movies, which contain simple themes, all posit that "Good is more powerful than Evil," and leave little room for doubt. Yes, the plucky protagonist must face numerous challenges before vanquishing his malignant foes, but the value of Harry's virtues are never in doubt, nor is the noxiousness of the villains' malevolence. On the other hand, more thematically complex (yet still commercial) films like *Signs* and *A Beautiful Mind* start with a question. In the case of *Signs*, that question is: "Is there divine order in the universe, or are our lives guided by mere chance?" *A Beautiful Mind* asks, "What is more important, genius or sanity?"

For the conflict to be effective, both sides must be equally weighted. For example, in *Signs*, Mel Gibson's ex-priest has every reason to deny — or at least doubt — the existence of God. He's experienced far too much personal tragedy to accept the notion of a just and almighty deity. His younger brother, played by Joaquin Phoenix, can argue equally effectively in favor of the existence of God based on his own personal faith. In *A Beautiful Mind*, mathematician John Nash is faced with an awful choice: Allow his genius to flourish at the expense of his sanity, or take the medications that will control his schizophrenia while at the same time clouding his unique brain. Both films — and hundreds like them — grip audiences by posing dilemmas whose answers are tantalizingly elusive.

Truly complex stories often end in ways that are emotionally and/or intellectually unsettling, or that overtly challenge the societal status quo. For example, *Mystic River* concludes with the most sympathetic characters either dead or communally ostracized, and justice definitely not done. Best Picture Oscar-winner *Chicago* ended with its protagonist not only literally getting away with murder, but ultimately being rewarded handsomely for her crime.

Complex themes make for great movies because real life is often complex, muddy, and unjust. You remember the story of Elian Gonzales, the Cuban boy rescued by fisherman off the Florida coast on Thanksgiving Day, 1999. His legal status became the subject of a heated national debate that lasted nearly half a year. On one hand, how could America deny this boy the freedoms we all enjoy? On the other hand, how can you deny a father the right to his own son — even if the guy was a Communist? Freedom vs. Fatherhood. Two values, equally weighted, suddenly at mortal odds. The ending to such a conflict could only be unsatisfying — which it was. Which is exactly why it made for such great drama.

Imbue *your* next script — be it a drama, a romance, or even a comedy — with such thematic complexity, and you stand a good chance of not only creating a unique and compelling screenplay, but launching your own lucrative screenwriting career.

TOO TRUE TO BE GOOD
When Reality and Fiction Collide

It's often said that truth is stranger than fiction — because fiction has to make sense. In fact, writing screenplays based on actual events, be they recent or historical, can prove to be a major challenge to any writer simply because real life tends not to follow the classic three-act structure that traditional storytelling demands.

Take the recent Iraq War, for example. Could you effectively tell that story as a movie? Sure, we have a wonderful villain in Saddam Hussein, but he barely registers on the radar after the onset of Act Two — if he was ever really there at all. And who's the hero? George W. Bush? Tommy Franks? Jessica Lynch? Michael Moore? And what about that great Act Three climax that any good story is supposed to lead up to? It's doubtful that the toppling of Saddam's statue ranks up there with, say, the destruction of the Guns of Navarone or the detonation of the dreaded Death Star. Finally, what's the denouement? What's the "new equilibrium" that the resolution establishes? As the late Chinese premier Mao Tse Tung so famously responded when asked to comment on the meaning of the French Revolution: "Too soon to tell."

Biographies, historical epics, and even contemporary "ripped-from-the-headlines" stories all pose similar challenges to the screenwriter. With the possible exception of legal cases, which have the benefit of the trial process to provide dramatic structure, few "true stories" fit neatly into the classic dramatic paradigm. Even harder is trying to write a dramatic story against the background of a sprawling dramatic event, such as a war or natural disaster.

Should you ever desire to face the challenges in writing cinematic "faction," here are some useful tips to remember:

If they're alive, you need the rights. Just because a story appears in a newspaper, magazine, or on television doesn't mean it's suddenly "public domain." To the contrary, although events, be they historical or timely, can never be proprietary, private lives are. If you want to write about anyone who's still alive, it's best to consult an attorney to see what rights need to be secured — and from whom — before proceeding. The same holds true for the recently deceased. For example, following the dramatic rescue of those nine Pennsylvania coal miners in 2002, agents, writers, and producers were all over Somerset County trying to snap up rights from anyone and everyone who was involved. The result was the 2002 MOW *The Pennsylvania Miners' Story.* (A creative title if there ever was one.) Likewise, writing partners Scott Alexander & Larry Karaszewski spent months pursing the rights to the life of the late Andy Kaufman before penning 1999's *Man on the Moon*, despite the fact that Kaufman died in 1984.

Narrow your story's scope. Tighter stories tend to be more powerful stories. When dealing with biographies or historical dramas, it's critical to find the smaller dramatic story within the larger true-life saga. For example, there's a reason why filmmakers tend to focus on individual missions or battles rather than trying to dramatize entire wars. Likewise, when writing about a famous person, it's best to focus on those incidents that actually made that person famous rather than trying to chronicle someone's life from birth to death.

It often helps to think of your true-life tale as a work of fiction. If you were making this story up, where would you begin? Where would you end? What incidents are the most important, and which can you safely ignore?

For example, when writing *Erin Brockovich*, Oscar-winning screenwriter Susannah Grant focused on how Erin got involved in, and eventually helped win, the class-action lawsuit against PG&E. What happened to her before and what has happened to her since are merely alluded to, rather than dramatized.

Narrow your cast of characters. When reading about a biographical film, you often find that certain key characters are "composites" of several others. This is because the incidental people in a person's life tend to be numerous, and drama demands economy. So, for example, when writing the story of a famous movie star, you may choose to give him or her a single agent rather than the half-dozen or more the subject may have had over the course of a real career. Likewise, famous personalities who in reality had numerous romantic partners, are usually restricted to just one or two in a dramatic presentation. (Which is exactly what Alexander & Karaszewski did with Courtney Love's character in *Man on the Moon*.) This brings us to a very important piece of advice:

Never let the facts get in the way of the truth. Recently, biographical pictures like *Hurricane* and *A Beautiful Mind* have been sharply criticized by some for deviating from the historical record. Horse-hockey. From Shakespeare to Spielberg, dramatists have always played fast-and-loose with the facts to spin a good yarn. And why not? The whole point of telling a story is to make a point, not to simply chronicle events. As a storyteller, your job is to have a point of view, and then to arrange the facts at hand to support that point of view in the most interesting and compelling way possible.

Which is why, for example, Oscar-winner Akiva Goldsman made the brilliant choice of writing the first half of *A Beautiful Mind* like a Cold War thriller, only at the midpoint revealing that the events we saw were a schizophrenic delusion. The fact that the real John Nash may have hallucinated about invading aliens, not nefarious Russians, wasn't the point; by making the hero's delusions plausible, Goldsman successfully brought us into the hero's mind and allowed us to share his fear and confusion. Had Goldsman stuck to the facts, the resulting episodes would have been so disconnected and absurd that we would have only been able to observe the character clinically and from a distance, rather than connecting with him as personally as we did.

Find the themes in real-life events. All too often, writers attempt to give their stories "scope" by setting them against an historical backdrop. However, if you're going to write a story *about* an event, it's critical to find a *theme* within that event and then construct your screen story — including your characters — accordingly. The best example of this is 1997's *Titanic*, written and directed by Oscar-winner James Cameron, which also just happens to be the most financially successful movie of all time.

The story of the sinking of the mighty White Star ocean liner has been told many times, but never with as much emotional power as it was in Cameron's version. This is because Cameron went beyond the obvious theme — *hubris* — and looked for something more compelling. Examining the historical record, Cameron saw that, of all 1,523 people who died that fateful night, a disproportionate number were from third class steerage. And there he found his thematic hook: class warfare. His story was not just going to be about classic arrogance, it was going to be about the rich versus the poor. In his not-so-veiled Marxian narrative, the rich would not only exploit the poor, but would also survive at the poor's expense.

Which was exactly the story he told. His hero was a poor but happy Bohemian (Jack Dawson) who falls in love with a rich but frustrated heiress (Rose DeWitt Bukater). And, playing the story of Titanic's passengers out in microcosm, the poor man, Jack, must ultimately die so that the rich girl, Rose, can live. (Of course, to soften the blow, Rose's family is merely faux-rich; the real villains are the truly wealthy.)

Identifying his story's theme gave Cameron his characters, his structure, and ultimately, his ending.

Far less successful was Randall Wallace's screenplay for *Pearl Harbor*. This is because, while an able writer, Wallace failed to identify what the Pearl Harbor attack was really about: *denial*. In 1941, America as a nation naively believed that it could ignore the evil that was enveloping the rest of the planet and somehow remain immune to it. America's leaders had ample evidence that war was inevitable, but the country as a whole simply refused to believe the obvious — until it was too late. Had Wallace written about *that* — about people doing everything possible to live in a dream world until being rudely forced to face harsh reality — his movie as a whole would probably have been a lot more interesting, and possibly more successful.

Clearly, writing about real life characters and events is often far more challenging than being able to spin a tale from whole cloth. But there are benefits, too. As Alexander and Karaszewski have noted when discussing their preference for off-the-wall biographies, when writing about actual people and events, no meddling studio exec can tell you to take out a scene because "something like that could never happen."

Truth is always the best defense.

NICE GUYS FINISH LAST
Being Bad Can Be Good for Your Feature Film Hero

"Embrace the dark side," Darth Vader tells young Luke Skywalker in 1983's *Return of the Jedi*. Similar advice could be given to contemporary screenwriters attempting to catch the eye of jaded studio executives, finicky film stars, and demanding audiences. Much to the Religious Right's chagrin, there's little room in modern Hollywood's production slate for squeaky clean heroes who stand for old-fashioned virtues, lead exemplary lives, and never have a hair out of place. No, from domineering and manipulative Charles Foster Kane in *Citizen Kane*, to the Humbert Humbert-like Lester Burnham in *American Beauty*, to the ruthless Jimmy Marcus in *Mystic River*, we like our dramatic protagonists dark, dangerous, and — to employ an overused word — edgy.

Of course, our culture's fascination with anti-heroes is hardly a twenty-first century phenomenon. From the earliest days of cinema, Hollywood has gleefully put "gray" characters at the center of its dramatic series. The filmographies of such Golden Era luminaries as Humphrey Bogart, Barbara Stanwyck, James Cagney, Bette Davis, Clark Gable, and Joan Crawford are rife with rogues, killers, tough guys, schemers, and smart alecks. Even the greatest comedians of that era — W.C. Fields, the Marx Brothers, and Mae West, to name just three — found fame and fortune by celebrating the less virtuous aspects of the human animal.

Today, stars like Mel Gibson, Bruce Willis, John Travolta, Robert De Niro, Nicolas Cage, Adam Sandler, Michael Douglas, and even Jim Carrey usually play characters who have as many negative qualities as positive ones. In October 1999, *TV Guide* listed its picks for "TV's 50 Greatest Characters Ever." Who nabbed the Number One spot? Why, *Taxi*'s Louie DePalma, played by Danny DeVito, who was described, in A-Z fashion, as "abrasive, base, crapulous, deceitful, embittered, fractious, galling, hard-hearted, ignoble, jaundiced, knavish, lecherous...." Yes, as any art student will tell you, the way you create dimension is through the use of shadow — and shadows are inevitably dark.

How can you employ the "dark side" to make your screenplay's hero more interesting? Here are a few suggestions:

Make him or her an outlaw. Let's get something straight up front: An outlaw is not necessarily a criminal. True, some dramatic protagonists, from *Little Caesar's* Caesar Enrico Bandello to *The Talented Mr. Ripley*'s Tom Ripley have, in fact, been killers, thieves, con men, etc., and such personalities *do* tend to make excellent cinematic fodder. But other "outlaws" have simply been men and women who live and work "outside the law" or the rules of conventional behavior. Extreme examples of "good" bad guys would be Robin Hood, Zorro, *The Matrix*'s Neo, and other rebels who stand up against repressive establishments. On a less grandiose scale, the characters played in the past by Humphrey Bogart and Marlon Brando, or more recently Jack Nicholson and Nicolas Cage, have simply been people who live by their own rules, consequences be damned.

Since it can be difficult to create prolonged sympathy for a true criminal, writers often find it useful to put their "outlaw" heroes in opposition to antagonists who are even more destructive and antisocial than *they* are. Films from *The Sting* to *Pulp Fiction* to *The Italian Job* have pitted bad guys against *really* bad guys in order to create heroes out of characters who might otherwise be cast in the antagonist role. In comedies, con men like Zero Mostel's Max Bialystock in *The Producers* or Jack Black's Dewey Finn in *School of Rock* win our sympathy by simply having wonderful dreams — dreams that mitigate the underhanded means they use to achieve them.

Give your hero an "inner demon." Nothing cuts a boring "good guy" down to size like a good character flaw. At best, this will be a weakness that gets the hero into trouble early in the story and then proceeds to cause as much, if not more, tsuris than the villain himself. Alcoholism, drug or sex addiction, phobias, suicidal tendencies, or any other compulsion you can come up with might be just the thing to give your character the "edge" studio execs, stars, and audiences are looking for.

Overcoming that "inner demon" then becomes the true point of your narrative, and that victory creates the "character arc" that development execs love to see in cinematic heroes.

Give your hero an attitude. Angry heroes with smart mouths and a healthy contempt for authority are cinematic staples, and there's no reason why you shouldn't take full advantage of the benefits this archetype affords. The classic icons of the Hollywood "tough guy" hero are, of course, Bogart and Cagney. Today, actors like Bruce Willis, Mel Gibson, and Will Smith usually portray similar iconoclastic characters. Tom Cruise has made an entire career out of playing "mavericks" who like to mouth off to authority figures.

Unfortunately, modern Hollywood has given us few equivalents for the equally smart-mouthed females of old, such as Barbara Stanwyck, Rosalind Russell, Bette Davis, Carole Lombard, and Katharine Hepburn. Maybe it's time you invented a new one?

Have your good guy go bad. Another effective approach to storytelling is to begin with an otherwise decent character and then place him or her in a situation in which he or she makes all the wrong decisions, thus testing the limits of his or her own virtue. Some recent examples of "good guy goes bad" stories include *A Simple Plan* and *Election*. Such stories tend to be as revelatory as they are entertaining since they force the audience to ask itself: "What would *I* do in circumstances like this?" In the end, such movies are inevitably morality tales.

Is there still room in Hollywood for a classic "hero"? Someone who doesn't kill, maim, steal, curse, drink, gamble, or diddle with fifteen-year-olds? Someone who stands for Mom, apple pie, truth, justice, and the American Way? Of course there is, but such characters can be dreary and dull if not placed in circumstances so compelling as to overcome such characters' lack of texture. Dark characters will *always* be more fascinating, if for no other reason than all people are made up of both bad and good, evil and virtue, and it is the struggle between these opposing forces that creates the human experience.

Besides, we understand Tom Hanks is already booked for the next decade.

A FEW BAD MEN
Creating Great Movie Villains

The late great Vincent Price once said that he had no trouble being typecast as a villain because, in movies, villains get to have all the fun. It's true that the villain is often the most colorful and multifaceted character in a motion picture. It can also be argued that it's the villain who often proves to be a movie's biggest attraction, who drives the narrative, who sets the agenda, and who ultimately defines what the movie is about.

Without Darth Vader, Luke Skywalker would still be harvesting water vapor on Tatooine. Without Hannibal Lecter, Clarice Starling would still be running laps at Quantico. Without Hans Gruber, John McClane would never have had to endure two vastly inferior *Die Hard* sequels. And let's be honest, no one goes to the Batman movies to see who's under the cowl. It's the bad guy roles that attract such A-list talents as Jack Nicholson, Michelle Pfeiffer, Jim Carrey, and Arnold Schwarzenegger.

Villains rule.

So what's the secret to creating a great movie villain? Here are some key ideas to keep in mind:

Villains need something really big to do. The larger and more dramatic the bad guy's objective, the greater and more interesting a threat he or she becomes. This is why James Bond villains inevitably want to either destroy or take over the world. Anything less is simply not worth 007's time. Serial killers are popular these days because they kill a lot, and are therefore more dramatic that the old-fashioned one-off Agatha Christie-style murderer.

Even if you're watching a more realistic drama or comedy, try to take the antagonist at least one step beyond. This inevitably makes the hero take extreme steps to thwart him or her, and therein lies the stuff of involving cinema.

Villains should be ruthless. Heroes must always follow certain codes of morality and common decency. Villains have no such restraints. They'll do anything they feel is necessary to achieve their ends, regardless of the pain and suffering they might ultimately cause. In fact, it is their very disregard for others that makes them villains. (The ultimate expression of this ruthlessness is James Cameron's *Terminator*, the true "unstoppable killer.")

Villains are inevitably slaves to their appetites. Whereas heroes are usually motivated by the need to see justice served or some other noble cause, villains go after things simply because they want them. They're motivated by greed, lust, and all those other deliciously deadly sins. Simply showing these characters pursuing their pleasures can turn an audience against them. For example, have you ever seen anything more stomach-turning than puffy old Joss Ackland making a play for fetching young Patsy Kensit in *Lethal Weapon 2*? That moment alone justified putting a bullet though his head.

Keep your villain active. Nothing is more boring than a bad guy who puts a plan in motion in Act One and then just sits and watches things play out for the rest of the film. A good villain should be always on the move, reacting to problems and trying new solutions — just like the hero.

Have your villain think he is the hero. A big mistake many writers make is to have their villains revel in their nastiness. Usually, this makes them come off as clichéd and melodramatic. Instead, remember that bad guys rarely think of themselves as "bad." They always have a reason for doing their dastardly deeds, a rationale for their foul, anti-social behaviors. In their own minds they are heroes — taking necessary measures to correct a perceived injustice, to exact revenge, or simply demonstrate their superiority over an inferior and undeserving world, i.e., Dennis Hopper in *Speed*. Shakespeare was a master of this, as evidenced by such sympathetic villains as *Othello*'s Iago, *The Merchant of Venice*'s Shylock, and *The Tempest*'s Caliban.

Give your villain a personal life. Even the most vile among us don't spend all our time being monstrous. We have jobs. Friends. Hobbies. Families. Extracurricular activities. Villains need them, too. Give your bad guy an activity that brings him pleasure. Show him "away from the office," indulging in some harmless pastime like fishing or playing the piano. In short, make him a person rather than merely an instrument of the plot.

Make your villain smart. Heroes are only as capable as their antagonists are, so it's critical that your bad guy be at least as smart as, if not smarter than, your lead. Drama needs complications and setbacks, and your antagonist is the person who has to provide them. Smart villains make for smarter movies.

Make your villain vulnerable. Just as there is nothing as boring as a hero who can't be killed, a villain without flaws is pretty much a snore. Norman Bates' insecurities and maternal obsession are what made him so interesting — not just his acumen with a kitchen knife. *It's a Wonderful Life's* Mr. Potter was rich and powerful and nasty as hell, but he was also old and physically impaired. Heck, even Darth Vader has to walk around in a portable iron lung. Give your villain some weaknesses, fears, and phobias, and your story will be better for it.

Villains need sufficient screen time. Many writers only cut to the villain when it's time for a plot point. Better writers spend the necessary time to flesh their villains out, to give them dimension, and to make them recognizable human beings. It's no coincidence that the *Batman* villains tend to get as much, if not more, screen time than the Caped Crusader himself. They're simply more interesting.

In 700 B.C., the epic poet Homer wrote that "Evil does not prosper." A lot has changed in the past 2,700 years. Not only does evil prosper, but it's big business. You may create a Sherlock Holmes, a James Bond, or an Indiana Jones. But if you can come up with a Freddy Krueger, your future is assured.

THE "X" FACTOR
Writing Strong Female Characters

Every year, especially around Academy Award season, we hear the same lament: "There aren't enough good parts for women these days." Those making these claims — usually actresses — have a legitimate case. Unlike the 1930s and 1940s when Hollywood divas like Bette Davis, Katherine Hepburn, Marilyn Monroe, Joan Crawford, and Barbara Stanwyck stood toe-to-toe with such male icons as Clark Gable, Humphrey Bogart, Spencer Tracey, and Errol Flynn, the track record of today's most bankable female stars — e.g. Julia Roberts, Cameron Diaz, Catherine Zeta-Jones, Drew Barrymore, Renée Zellweger, et al — is arguably less impressive than that racked up by Tom Cruise, Mel Gibson, Denzel Washington, Russell Crowe, Sean Penn, and others on the male A-List.

Part of the blame for this disparity can be placed on the audience, which has exhibited a clear preference for films with decidedly male themes. (Numerous studies have shown that it's far easier for a man to convince a woman to see a high-testosterone action picture than it is for a woman to persuade a man to see a "chick flick.") On the other hand, the seemingly universal preference for "guy films" — especially on the increasingly vital world market — may simply be the result of the paucity of good female-oriented movies being written and produced.

Whether you are writing a movie with a female lead or a male-oriented film with female co-stars, it's still extremely important to write strong, solid female characters. You owe it to your actors. You owe it to your audience. And you certainly owe it to the readers and production executives who will be the first to evaluate your spec script — at least half of whom are likely to be women.

Ironically, many women have just as much trouble writing good female characters as do men — not because they don't understand female psychology, but because they fail to use that understanding to create a character who is, in fact, cinematic. Both male and female screenwriters need to learn to write female characters who are strong, original, and multi-dimensional — then place these characters in stories that allow these attributes to be realized.

Like everything else in Hollywood, it ain't easy.

Let's begin by reviewing those characteristics that define a strong cinematic character, regardless of sex. These are the things actors, producers, directors — and audiences — want to see in their heroes and heroines:

Goals: First and foremost, a hero has to *want* something. It's the hero's goal that gives the story direction and purpose. Very often, the hero's goal *changes* during the course of the movie — this change is usually what defines the end of Act One — but a goal is always present nonetheless. It's equally important for your antagonist to have a goal, be that person male or female. Usually the hero and antagonist's goal conflict, which is what makes the story interesting.

Think of the best female roles of the past five years. Julia Roberts as Erin Brockovich? She had a goal: First to simply get a job, and then to bring justice to the citizens being injured by the pollutants secretly released into the environment by Pacific Gas & Electric. Renée Zellweger as Roxie Hart in *Chicago*? She wanted to be a vaudeville star. Diane Keaton in *Something's Gotta Give?* First she wanted to maintain her emotional independence, then find a way to deal with the heartbreak caused by her loss of Jack Nicholson's Harry Sanborn.

A character without a goal — be it male or female — is inherently a boring character. And to be cinematic, that goal must be something that can lead to *conflict*. This is why scripts about women striving for "self-realization" — and hundreds of them are written every year — make for poor cinema. Your heroine (or supporting character) has to want something that has consequences beyond herself.

Passion: Your heroine must not only want something important, she must want it badly enough that she's willing to take enormous risks to achieve her goal. Passion is what usually distinguishes lead roles from supporting ones. A heroine is willing to face danger

STORYTELLING

— be it physical or emotional — whereas a secondary or tertiary character is not. (And when a secondary character *does* willingly face danger, what do we call this behavior? *Heroic!*)

Passion usually translates into action, and the willingness to take action is what Hollywood looks for in a strong dramatic character, male *or* female.

Weaknesses: A dramatic character cannot be invulnerable, or there isn't any possibility of conflict. In addition to a character's goals and passions, we want to know her fears and weaknesses. And we not only want to be *told* about these fears and weaknesses, but we want them to be an integral part of your story. We want to see them played out *on screen*.

For many writers — women as well as men — the temptation is to overemphasize the female character's fears and weaknesses (e.g., the classically hysterical "damsel in distress," or the girl who weeps at the slightest provocation), just as it is to ignore them when writing male characters. The trick to writing good female *and* male roles is to bring the two into balance, to show enough weakness that the hero's success is constantly in doubt, while also imbuing the character with enough strength so that his or her triumph is both believable and satisfying.

Unique talents/idiosyncrasies: To make a character of either gender unusual — or even unique — you should give them one or more special talents or bits of idiosyncratic behavior that emphasize his or her individuality. For example, in Nancy Meyer's screenplay for *Something's Gotta Give*, Diane Keaton's character is a very successful Broadway playwright. She's able to artistically communicate her hopes, fears, and ideas in dramatic form. In 1998's *The Mask of Zorro*, the film that put Catherine Zeta-Jones on the map, her character was not only an extreme beauty but also an expert dancer and fencer. Her tango with Antonio Bandaras and subsequent "duel" with his masked alter-ego were arguably the two most memorable moments of that film. The best film characters are those with unusual talents or abilities, who are given a chance to express those attributes in memorable ways.

So far, we've discussed how female characters are little different from male ones. Now let's talk about how they are different. And, yes, they *are* different. While there are a few examples of actresses successfully playing roles that were originally written for men (Sigourney Weaver as Ripley in the original *Alien*, for example), by far the best female roles are those that emphasize those characteristics that make women women. And we're not just talking about the physical ones.

Action — direct vs. indirect: As a group, women tend to prefer indirect action to the more direct male approach. For example, while a man will say to his wife, "Honey, get me a beer," a woman will say, "Honey, I'm thirsty," and expect her husband to figure out the action necessary to satisfy her need. To engage a single woman, a man will traditionally walk up and just start talking. To engage a man, a woman may simply give him a flirtatious look, smile, and then turn away to encourage him to approach *her*.

There are no value judgments associated with this difference. One approach is not necessarily "better" than the other. They are just different. And both can be equally effective.

Verbal vs. physical: Although women are certainly *capable* of physical violence, it should not be their preferred response. It's no surprise that a female agent is used to interrogate the unflappable Dr. Hannibal Lecter in *The Silence of the Lambs* (a role for which Jodie Foster won an Academy Award for Best Actress), that a female psychologist is used to get into the mind of a comatose serial killer in *The Cell*, or that it's a female therapist who treats crime boss Tony Soprano in HBO's *The Sopranos*. Men blow things up. Women talk. And they often do it better than men.

Regarding of female-oriented action movies, their record has been spotty at best — at least so far. Sigourney Weaver in the *Alien* movies worked, Linda Hamilton in *Terminator 2* kicked ass, and the first *Charlie's Angels* earned big bucks, but otherwise the Hollywood landscape is littered with dozens of failed attempts to establish a viable female action hero in the Stallone/Willis/Schwarzenegger mold. Even the Lara Croft series never took off the way its creators had hoped.

It might be argued that the *way* women fight on screen needs to be different than the way men fight. Men shoot guns. They fly airplanes. Their violence is, for the most part, distant and detached. Women, on the other hand, are at their best when the fight is up close and personal. (Police data reveals that men prefer to kill with guns, while for women the knife is the weapon of choice.)

The tradition of the "lethal weapon" female action hero took off in the 1960s with the hand-to-hand karate action of Emma Peel in TV's *The Avengers*. The battling babes in *Charlie's Angels* (both the

TV and movie versions) continued this preference for intimate action, and even Uma Thurman — in both volumes of *Kill Bill* — preferred the blade to the bazooka.

The bottom line: Women want to see the pain in their victims' eyes. Men just want to blow things up real good.

Again, these differences are not ones of value, merely of style. Recognizing and exploiting these cultural and biological differences while adhering to the universal rules of good story-telling will allow you to create strong, memorable female characters that both women and men can enjoy.

DESIGNING WOMEN
How Real Men Write Real Women

"I think of a man. Then I take away reason and accountability."

That's how best-selling novelist Melvin Udall (Jack Nicholson) explained his secret for writing great female characters in 1997's Academy Award-winning dramedy *As Good As It Gets*. Fortunately, most successful screenwriters don't follow Udall's formula, for if they did we'd never have met Isla Lund (*Casablanca*), Margo Channing (*All About Eve*), or Clarice Starling (*The Silence of the Lambs*) — not to mention Annie Hall, Dana Scully, Buffy the Vampire Slayer, and countless other fictional females who are now part of our cultural pantheon.

So how do you write credible females? It's a problem that daunts many a male screenwriter. For despite considerable gains by women over the past thirty years, the vast majority of professional screen scribes continue to be men. And most men remain uncertain about — if not downright intimidated by — female psychology.

For those of you interested in creating women who are more than just objects of sexual desire or screaming targets of knife-wielding maniacs, here are some concepts that may help you in your quest to create women who are emotionally, psychologically, and dramatically complete.

The requirements of drama are universal. Male or female, all dramatic characters are built on a common foundation. First and foremost, your female character must have a goal, something she's trying to accomplish in the story. Your character must have specific abilities, but also specific limits, fears, and weaknesses. Your character also needs a unique temperament. Is she optimistic or pessimistic? Compulsive or deliberate? Even-keeled or emotionally volatile? Don't be afraid to imbue your character with contradictory temperaments. A person can be jovial one moment and depressed the next, depending on the circumstances.

Lady Macbeth lives. All dramatic characters have to want something. But how men and women pursue their goals is often very different. A few years back, researchers performed an experiment in which children were put in a room with a toy placed behind a mesh divider. The little boys hurled themselves against the divider until it fell down and they could get the toy. But the little girls took a different approach: They cried their heads off until someone got the toy for them. The end results were the same, but the strategies were fundamentally different. And these behaviors tend to continue into adult life.

While men usually act directly, women will often employ surrogates — typically male ones. Many classic film noirs are based on this truism. For example, in noirs like *Double Indemnity*, *The Postman Always Rings Twice*, *Body Heat*, and *The Last Seduction*, the scheming female protagonist first seduces a male dupe, then convinces him to commit murder — a murder from which she benefits, but for which he ultimately takes the fall. (You almost never see these roles reversed.)

Women talk. Recently, medical science has confirmed what many people have long suspected — that women's brains contain larger language sections than do men's. As a result, women are more inclined to talk their way through problems, whereas men — being the dumb rocks we are — tend to prefer direct physical action.

In terms of drama, this means that you'll approach a crisis situation differently if you're waiting one who is male. This is true for action movies as well as dramatic ones. For example, take a situation in which two cops — one male, one female — show up at a bank where a robber is holding a dozen people hostage. If you're going to write this realistically, the female cop will favor negotiation; the male may be instinctively inclined to try to take the robber out through violence. (In real life, female police officers are preferred over males in domestic violence situations for this very reason. And this doesn't mean that male police officers won't attempt to negotiate, or that the female cops aren't capable of blowing the bad guy's head off. It just means that their gut instincts will likely be different, and this will color their ultimate choices of action.)

Women also seem to be more inclined to seek emotional validation through social interaction. This means that they're not only more likely to confide in their own sex as are men, but they have a need to know that other women feel the way they do. This is why in such modern "chick flicks" as *Sleepless in Seattle*, *Waiting to Exhale*, *The First Wives Club*, and *Mona Lisa Smile*, you find scenes in which women sit around talking about how they feel, and seeking communion with their contemporaries.

(When men behave this way, it is usually for comedic effect, as in 1997's *In & Out*, where such intimacy is mocked as effeminate.)

Make sure your female character has some kind of support group, and give her time to express her emotions.

Don't underestimate the maternal instinct. For eons, women have traditionally been care-givers and protectors of the young, and this pattern continues to this day. In movies, you often find women concerned principally with protecting their families and children (Renée Zellweger in *Jerry Maguire*, Helen Hunt in *As Good As It Gets*). You can even get away with putting a woman in a pure action role, as long as she's busting heads *for the children*. Examples of this include Sigourney Weaver in *Aliens*, Linda Hamilton in *Terminator 2: Judgment Day*, and Jodie Foster in *Panic Room*.

Women are individuals. Although women share certain group characteristics, the fact remains that every person is an individual, and it is this individuality that makes a character — any character — interesting. You need to give your principle female characters interests, desires, hobbies, and talents that are unusual, unexpected, and colorful. Avoid stereotypes like the Dumb Blonde, the Meek Housewife, or the Hooker with a Heart of Gold. Above all else, make certain your characters possess a passion for something. It is that overwhelming, unstoppable desire that will drive a story forward — regardless of a character's chromosomes.

SIZZLING SIDEKICKS
Creating First-Class Second Bananas

In virtually all screenwriting books, courses, and seminars, significant attention is paid to creating strong, sympathetic, proactive heroes and equally strong, detestable, seemingly unstoppable villains. But what about the secondary roles? The supporting characters? The second bananas? Would Sherlock Holmes have endured for more than a century without Dr. Watson? Would Superman look so super if not contrasted with that schlep, Jimmy Olson? And how far would the Lone Ranger have gotten in the Old West without Tonto?

Yes, in literature, television, and motion pictures, good supporting characters are often critical to a story's success, as well as its memorability. But they're a sub-species of dramatic personae often overlooked — or even dismissed — by both writers and pundits. (As Bill Murray so memorably put it when predicting Best Supporting Oscar winners on *SNL*, "*Who cares!*")

Don't be misled. Your screenplays need more than just heroes and villains to be viable. In fact, without supporting characters to challenge the protagonist's values, provide guidance, and serve as bad examples, most heroes would operate in intellectual, emotional, and spiritual vacuums. With this in mind, let's examine the key roles supporting characters often play, and how to make these characters as interesting as your leads.

The human ear trumpet: One of the most valuable roles a supporting character often plays is that of a sounding board. He or she exists to give the hero or villain someone to talk to, a vehicle through which the primary character can express his or her thoughts, emotions, plans, etc., and thus provides the audience with information critical to the story. (Unlike novels and short stories, movies and television shows don't have the luxury of the internal monologue.) In classic drama, the role of Horatio in Shakespeare's *Hamlet* is often cited as such a passive, albeit critical "Human Ear Trumpet." Two extreme modern examples would be the decapitated noggin that was the centerpiece of Sam Peckinpah's *Bring Me the Head of Alfredo Garcia* and "Wilson," the anthropomorphic volleyball in *Cast Away*; without these "characters," the heroes would just be talking to empty air.

Of course, if you intend to make your supporting characters *human* ear trumpets and not inanimate objects, it helps to give them a little life of their own. This usually means:

Providing them with a naturally intimate relationship with the leading character, such as a that of family member, friend, co-worker, etc.

Giving them a personality that either compliments or contrasts with the hero's/villain's. "Junior" versions of the leads serve as sympathetic and encouraging sounding boards, whereas mirror images are able to play devil's advocate and challenge all of the leading character's assumptions.

Allowing them to have agendas of their own. This is the element most often missing from underwritten supporting roles: individual motive. Even human ear trumpets need to have their own hopes, dreams, fears, and ambitions, and the more you texture your second banana with these elements, the better your screenplay as a whole becomes.

The mentor: The role of teacher/guide is critical to many dramatic tales, especially those that follow the popular Joseph Campbell's "Hero With a Thousand Faces" paradigm. From Merlin in the Arthurian legends to Abbe Faria in *The Count of Monte Cristo* to Obi-Wan Kenobi in *Star Wars* to Gandolf in *The Lord of the Rings* trilogy, the role of the wise old sage has been critical to classic storytelling.

By definition, mentors are knowledgeable, experienced, capable, and concerned for the hero's well-being. They also tend to be strict, sometimes impatient task-masters capable of occasional abuse. (Drill sergeants often play this role to the hilt in military pictures like *An Officer and a Gentleman* and *Full Metal Jacket*).

But the key to a truly memorable mentor is the element of *failure*. Virtually all great mentors suffer defeat at some point in their lives, often leaving them angry and embittered. It is therefore incumbent upon the hero to succeed where the mentor has failed, and thereby reverse their roles by the story's end.

The one who knows: This supporting character is similar to the mentor, although it's usually a smaller role and one that is less personally intimate with the hero. "The one who knows" is anyone — male or female — with information critical to the hero, someone who holds the key to his or her success and yet is often reclusive, unreachable, or just plain unreliable. "The one who knows" is often a key character in horror and science fiction movies. Usually a scientist, specialist, or someone who has encountered "the monster" in the past, this is the person who provides backstory and technical information necessary for forward progress. Such a character often remains a mystery figure — sometimes literally hidden in shadow — until he or she either pops up or is sought out when most needed.

It's often lots of fun to write — and play — "the one who knows," since these characters tend to be weird, eccentric, and filled with tics and idiosyncrasies. Again, like the mentor, "the one who knows" has usually suffered defeat or humiliation in the past, and tends to have a very dark side despite any comic characteristics that may exist on the surface. When writing such a character, be careful to introduce him or her early enough in the story so that when his or her function is revealed, he or she doesn't appear to just be a convenient *deus ex machina*.

The alter ego: This is perhaps the most important role a supporting character can play in a complex comedy or drama. Usually similar to the hero in the most important aspects, the alter ego exists to serve as a cautionary example for the protagonist caught in some kind of moral or ethical dilemma.

Examples of alter egos include Lisa Rowe (Angelina Jolie) in *Girl, Interrupted*; Cypher (Joe Pantoliano) in *The Matrix*, Sid Worley (David Keith) in *An Officer and a Gentleman*, and Tommy deVito (Joe Pesci) in *Goodfellas*. All of these characters bear superficial similarities to the hero, are either friends or co-workers of the hero, and find themselves in similar personal positions. The difference is, the alter ego inevitably succumbs to a temptation also being faced by the hero, and pays a terrible price as a result. This gives the hero the "kick" he or she needs to change his or her ways and start down the proper moral path.

Clearly, supporting characters play key roles in dramatic structure. Properly written, their impact can reverberate throughout an entire movie, even given a limited amount of exposure. For instance, it's interesting to note that several Best Supporting Oscar winners, such as Ned Beatty in *Network*, Meryl Streep in *Kramer vs. Kramer*, and Judi Dench in *Shakespeare in Love*, won their awards for performances that involved less than fifteen minutes of actual screen time.

MECHANICS

GREAT EXPECTATIONS
Getting Your Reader to Go All the Way

"Let's hit the ground running," said President-elect Ronald Reagan describing how he planned to take immediate action following his 1981 inauguration. The Gipper, himself a product of Hollywood, no doubt knew a thing or two about the importance of getting a story off to a fast start. Things haven't changed all that much in the last fifteen years. Throwing an audience right into the action is still the best way to engage their attention, whether it's a finished motion picture or just words on the printed page.

Most development executives will tell you that they more or less make up their minds about a spec screenplay's viability by page ten. If they're not hooked by that point — if something isn't happening that piques their interest — they figure chances are the story never will take flight. And you know what? Nine times out of ten, they'll be right.

This isn't to say that you have to launch immediately into your main conflict, or that your story can't unfold in a slower, more measured fashion. In fact, more often than not, you'll need the full thirty or so pages traditionally allotted to Act One to establish all the necessary information — to "lay the track" as it were — in order to make the rest of the movie work. But a good writer will make this initial exposition period just as interesting as the main body of the film. How do you do that? Simple: You have interesting people do interesting things.

Here are some tired-and-true tricks you can use to get your story up to speed in the first ten pages:

Open with your main character in motion. Since the days of Aristotle, characters have been defined by their actions. And, in drama, "action" is defined as a character doing what he or she feels is necessary to reach a specific goal.

A mistake many novice writers make is having their heroes static through most of Act One until, twenty-five minutes or so into the movie, something occurs — the classic "First Act Plot Point" — that forces them into motion. This is too little, too late. It's far more effective to open with your hero trying to solve a problem that defines who and what he or she is. This problem need not be related to what the story will ultimately be about, but should at least give the audience a sense that this person is already trying to move from Point A to Point B.

For example, if your hero is a cop, show us how he handles a violent perpetrator. Does he prefer violent action or steely negotiation? If she's a surgeon, show us how she deals with a medical emergency. Is she nervous or self-assured, emotionally involved or coldly distant? If your lead is a high school aged kid, you might open him with confronting some classroom bullies, girding himself to ask a pretty girl to the prom, or cleverly cheating on a difficult test. The particulars depend on the type of person your hero is and the needs of your unique story. The one common thread among all these examples is that something is always happening.

The 2003 animated mega-hit *Finding Nemo* has a great opening movement; in the first ten pages, the hero, Marlin (voiced by Albert Brooks), makes a plan to raise his family, loses in wife and 99 percent of his offspring to a raiding barracuda, takes his young son to his first day of school, then watches in terror as his only child is "kidnapped" by human divers. Here, we're given all the background we need to understand the character, his emotional turmoil and why he's so bound and determined to do whatever is necessary to bring his son home. It's a textbook example of storytelling efficiency.

Open with your villain in motion. Most action movies are driven more by their antagonists than by their heroes. It's the bad guy who has the goal and sets the agenda; the hero is just there to stop him at all costs.

Many successful action pictures begin with the villain taking the first step in his plan. Examples include Dennis Hopper killing the inquisitive janitor with a screwdriver in the first scene of *Speed*, Darth Vader and his Imperial Star Destroyer pursuing the Rebel blockade runner in *Star Wars*, or the title character murdering the punk for his clothes in the original *Terminator*. All of these actions immediately establish the nature of the conflict to come, before the hero is even introduced.

Open with a grabber that immediately draws us into the story. This is a dramatic incident (sometimes violent) that raises a number of questions that demand to be answered. A good example of this is the opening scene from 1987's *Lethal Weapon*. The film opens with a lovely aerial view of Los Angeles during Christmas season. We find a young woman standing on the balcony of a high-rise apartment building. Suddenly, she leaps to her death. Who was this woman? Why did she kill herself? And who's going to clean up the mess? Inquiring minds want to know — and so will your audience.

Instead of a traditional dramatic scene, you may opt to open with a montage or a set-piece. Sometimes narrated, such as in 1989's *Field of Dreams*, such scenes quickly and efficiently fill us in on the story's background. 1983's *The Big Chill* used a series of mini-scenes, in which we're quickly introduced to several characters, all of whom are doing something in a character-specific way.

Very often, such montages double as title and credit sequences. Beware: don't actually "call" for such a sequence in your screenplay. Where to put opening titles — if at all — is directorial decision, and directors hate it when writers presume to dictate such things. However, a well-placed, well-written opening montage clearly suggests such a sequence, allowing you to get what you want without actually calling for it.

To reiterate, the first ten pages of your screenplay should find your lead characters already in motion. Use their actions to tell us who and what they are. Introduce conflict as early as possible. Try to make your opening visually as well as dramatically interesting — an element of mystery is always effective.

It's been said that we live in an MTV-paced world. Certainly many modern movies reflect the speed and urgency of music videos. (It's no coincidence that many of today's top feature directors were weaned on videos and commercials.) But this is really nothing new. Four decades ago, Director Alfred Hitchcock described movies as "life with all the boring parts taken out." That's the key to a great first ten pages — and a great movie. Keep things moving. Focus on conflict.

And hit the ground running.

YOUR MISSION
Get In, Get To the Point, Get Out

Less is more when describing the professional screenwriter's approach to writing descriptive prose. The more information you can convey in the fewest possible words, the better your chances that the people reading your work will, in fact, pay attention. (When you're up against a $60/script reader who has to get through six specs before 10 a.m. Monday, this is no easy task.)

While working to keep your prose short, you also want to make it powerful. You want to use words that effectively communicate the action, tone, and imagery you see in your mind's eye. Your objective in writing cinematic prose is to emulate, as closely as possible, the actual movie-going experience. (This is one of the factors that makes screenwriting vastly different from other creative media, particularly novels. When writing a novel, you're free to take as much time as you want describing people, places, and objects. You can, if you wish, spend page upon page dwelling on minor details, all the while keeping your reader entranced with your prodigious prose. You have no such luxury when writing for the screen. In a screenplay, you need to make your point and get on with it!)

Here are some techniques you can use to make your descriptive prose more readable, and thereby more effective:

Keep your verbs in the active, present tense. In other words, avoid "-ing" verbs. Instead of "Joe is walking down the street" and "Jane is driving her car," say "Joe walks down the street" and "Jane drives her car." This is more immediate and punchy.

Avoid the verb "to be." Rather than repeatedly using "is" and "are," find verbs that are more descriptive and colorful. Example: Instead of writing "Joe is in the house," try something like "Joe putters around the house" or "Joe paces the room." (Characters do more, after all, than just exist.) Even something as simple as "Jane is at the wheel of the car" can be made more colorful, more visual by saying, "Jane steers through heavy traffic" or "Jane expertly pilots the vehicle." The length of the sentence is the same, but the image is more vivid.

Avoid over-using "begins to" and "starts to." Usually, these modifiers can be jettisoned with no ill effects. For example, it's usually better to write "Joe eats his meal" instead of "Joe starts to eat his meal," or "Mary crosses the street," instead of "Mary begins to cross the street." The exception to this is when, say, "Mary begins to cross the street...and gets hit by a bus."

Keep your sentences short and simple. Avoid run-on sentences. Frequent appearances by the word "and" is a good warning sign that your prose is getting ungainly. (Bad example: "Joe jumps into his car and pulls out his keys and jams them into the ignition and fires up the engine, then peels off in a cloud of dust." Good example: "Joe jumps into his car. Pulls out his keys. Jams them into the ignition. Fires up the engine and pulls away in a cloud of dust.")

When writing complex action, favor bullet sentences. As in the example above, this usually means dropping the subject nouns off all but the first sentence in a sequence. Here's another example of "bullet sentences" at work:

> Lt. Trench spots the fugitives' car. He hits his siren. Floors the accelerator. Jerks the steering wheel violently as he races to keep up with the perpetrators.

On the other hand, don't leave out articles like, "a," "the," "his," etc. This approach leads to choppy, unnatural Boris Badanov-style writing. For example:

> Lt. Trench spots fugitives' car. He hits siren. Floors accelerator. Jerks steering wheel violently as he races to catch up to perpetrators.

When in doubt, read your script out loud. If your writing is easy to speak, it's probably easy to read. On the other hand, if you have to struggle to speak your prose, or if it feels unnatural, then the reader will likely have difficulty with it as well.

Whenever possible, write *down* the page. Good screenwriting prompts the reader's eye to read down rather than across the page. This can be achieved in a number of ways. One is "stacking," which involves literally laying short sentences atop each other. Here's how the paragraph above looks "stacked:"

Lt. Trench spots the fugitives' car.
He hits the siren.
Floors the accelerator.
Jerks the steering wheel violently.
Races to catch up with the perpetrators.

Notice that it was necessary to break up the paragraph's last sentence to avoid a "wrap-around," a sentence that occupies more than one line. "Wrap-arounds" are aesthetically awkward in "stacked" paragraphs. (Note: Restrict "stacking" to action sequences or other similarly "percussive" events. The overuse of this technique not only diminishes its effect, but also artificially inflates your script's page length.)

Another, and infinitely subtler way to force a reader's eye down, is to end each line with a word or phrase that begs a question, leaving the reader's mind momentarily dangling and looking for an answer or modifier. Again using the above description, it could be rewritten like this:

Lt. Trench spots the fugitives' car. He hits the
siren. Floors the accelerator. Jerks the
steering wheel violently as he races to catch up with
the perpetrators.

This is a difficult technique to master, often forcing you to artificially restructure your sentences or leave unattractive spaces at the end of some sentences while you strive to achieve the desired effect. However, when done properly, it can aid in speeding the reader along — labeling your script as a "fast read."

Observe the four-line rule. Readers like to see a lot of white space on the page. When they see too many words, they often just skip ahead to the next dialogue block, sometimes missing key action moments. To avoid this, keep your copy blocks four lines or less. Not four sentences — four *lines*. If a paragraph ends up occupying more than four lines of text, break it up. Make it *look* like there's less to read.

KEEPING IT MOVING
The Art and Science of Dramatic Pacing

Harry Cohn, the despotic head of Columbia Pictures during the 1930s and 1940s, often said that he knew a picture was in trouble if, when watching it, he began to shift in his seat. This ultimately prompted the famous rejoinder from *Citizen Kane* co-writer Herman Mankiewicz: "Imagine — the whole world wired to Harry Cohn's ass!"

The issue of cinematic pacing — and its affects on the human derriere — is just as problematic today as it was sixty years ago, and its solution remains equally elusive. The reason why pacing is more art than science is because pacing is not about elapsed time; it's about how that time is *perceived* by the viewer. Pacing cannot be measured, it can only be *felt*. As we all know, a well-paced three-hour-long film can seem to move like lightning, whereas a poorly made thirteen-minute short can seem interminable. The key question: What distinguishes a well-paced story from a plodding one, and what techniques can we, as screenwriters, employ to help create the former and not the latter?

Before we can explore the subject of pacing, we have to recognize that we screenwriters are not wholly in control of the pacing process. Cinematic pacing is ultimately determined by directors who first shoot their scenes in a certain way and then supervise the assembly of those scenes in the editing room. What we as writers *can* do is set the stage for a well-paced movie by writing screenplays that are themselves well-paced and that *suggest* the best rhythms for the ultimate filmed product. (Of course, writing a well-paced script can be its own reward as it will tend to excite the reader — i.e., the story analyst, producer, and/or studio executive — and thus make him or her more likely to actually *buy* it!)

Here, then, are some suggestions on how to control and improve the pacing of your screenplay at all levels.

Pacing the movie as a whole. In most cases, good pacing requires the writer to adhere to the classic "Three Act Structure." Act One (the set up) should occupy approximately the first quarter of the screenplay, Act Two (story development) should occupy approximately the middle half, and Act Three (climax and resolution) should occupy approximately the final quarter. Is this formula written in stone? No, of course not. It only holds true about 98 percent of the time. Why does this structure work in the vast majority of cases? That's difficult to quantify. Suffice it to say that it just *feels* right. Maybe it's a matter of training; it's the way we've been *taught* to see movies. However, the more likely explanation is that, over the last century, many different dramatic structures have been tried and this one has proven to be the most successful (call it Dramatic Darwinism). In any case, it works. Make your first act much shorter than the recommended 25 percent and it will feel rushed. Make it much longer and the story starts to drag. Likewise, abbreviate the climax and the story feels unfinished, whereas if you extend it, it starts to feel padded. Regardless of your screenplay's length — 12 pages, 120 pages, or 240 pages — the Three Act Structure works. Don't mess with success.

Pacing your first act. Today's audience — the so-called MTV Generation — is known for its short attention span, and the stereotype is not too far off the mark. Today's films *are* paced faster than those of decades past, particularly in their first acts. First and foremost, you want to get your story off to a running start. Begin with people and things in motion. If you're opening with your hero, open with him or her *doing something* (preferably something that quickly establishes his or her character). Likewise, if you're opening with your villain, begin with him or her in the midst of doing something dastardly. In most cases, this opening sequence is *not* what the movie is eventually about, although it may have echoes in subsequent plot development. It's there to establish the hero's *status quo* and serve as the physical and psychological baseline for the adventure to come.

The next major step is the first plot point. It's the moment your hero's world is shaken up, requiring him or her to come up with a new objective and plan of action. In older discussions of screen structure, this first plot point was synonymous with the end of Act One and usually occurred on or around page 30 or so in a traditional 120-page screenplay. This is too late. In a well-paced contemporary script, the first plot point should occur somewhere between pages 20 and 25, the rest of Act One occupied by the hero first *reacting* to the invasion of his or her status quo and then formulating the new objective and plan of action. Some writers even manage to put their first plot point *before* the twentieth page, but this can be awkward as it gives the audience little time to get to know the hero and his or her world before things get shaken up.

Pacing your second act. Act Two pacing is usually where most screenwriters, even high-priced A-List writers, get into trouble. An hour is a lot of time to fill, and keeping audiences interested over such a prolonged span can challenge even the most skillful dramatist. The secret is to divide the second Act One into equal halves. In the beginning of Act Two, the hero, armed with his or her new objective and plan, struggles to achieve his or her new goal. This should lead to a "false climax" right around the midpoint, at which point one of two things usually happens: (1) The hero fails, forcing him or her to develop a wholly new plan-of-action, or (2) The hero succeeds, only to discover that the problem is a lot bigger than he or she initially imagined and, again, a whole new plan of action is required.

Pacing your third act. Act Three pacing usually involves "revving up" for the final confrontation, and then a prolonged battle scene (which can be physical or verbal) that ends with the hero's ultimate triumph or defeat. A short "cooling down" period (formally called the *denouement)*, follows, during which a new status quo is established. Take care to make your Act Three battle long enough to deliver maximum dramatic impact, but not so long that it becomes tedious. In a thirty-page third act, a climactic battle lasting ten to fifteen pages is usually ideal.

Pacing sequences: A "sequence" is a series of scenes all directed toward a single goal. Often synonymous with a "set-piece," a sequence is commonly a "movie-within-in-a-movie" in which the hero sets out to solve a specific problem/reach a single goal, encounters a series of obstacles, and then either succeeds or fails in his or her quest. Most sequences have the illusion of occurring in real time, that is, five minutes on the screen is the equivalent of five minutes in real life. In most modern action films, action sequences occur on an average of once every eight pages and tend to be anywhere from four to six pages in length. The intervening pages are occupied by dialogue/action that develops character and/or actually advances the plot. This same formula tends to work just as well for comedies and dramas. Concentrate on the set-pieces and keep expository/developmental scenes to a minimum.

Pacing scenes: For decades, the rule of thumb is that a movie is basically a series of sixty separate two-minute scenes. That's not too far off the mark. While it's true that some scenes can be as short as just a few seconds and others can go on for several minutes, on average, a motion picture scene is about two minutes long. That's the equivalent of two written pages. How long can a scene be? Again, the rule of thumb is: Don't go beyond four pages. Scenes *can* be longer than four minutes long, but they need a damned good reason for being so. A lot has to be happening within those four-plus pages to justify taking up so much real estate.

To keep individual scenes as "tight" as you can, you should always enter a scene as late as possible and exit as early as possible. For example, in one scene, two cops could agree to interview a crime witness. Unless you want to throw dramatically relevant obstacles in the cops' way, the next scene should begin with the cops already talking to the witness. No introductions. No bits of character "business." No showing the cops driving through the city and looking for the right address. Just get straight to the facts. TV's long-running *Law & Order* franchise is paced this way, and it's proven to be an audience-pleaser for more than a decade.

Pacing dialogue: In movies, scenes need to move fast, and dialogue needs to be just as fast. There's nothing as tedious as reading a screenplay in which one character talks for half a page, then another character talks for half a page, etc., etc. Real people usually don't talk this way, and neither should your characters. Most dialogue blocks should be only one or two sentences long. Some lines can consist of just a few words or sentence fragments. Dialogue should alternate quickly between characters, and it's often useful, especially in emotionally charged situations, to have characters actually interrupt one another. To really supercharge dialogue, have it overlap (the Howard Hawks technique). Have several conversations go on at once and people talk over one another. Have ever read a transcript of an actual real-life conversation? This is the way real people really talk.

Varying the pace: Nothing is more monotonous that a steady rhythm. Even a rhythm that is fast-paced can become numbing after just a few minutes. That's why you want to vary the length and complexity of the scenes within your screenplay. Break long sequences up with several short ones. After a kinetic action sequence, let your characters — and the audience — stop for a minute or so to catch their collective breath. You can even stop the action entirely for a few "beats" to give your characters time to think — or do nothing.

Varying the direction: Finally, you can improve your sense of pacing by regularly changing the direction in which your story seems to be headed. Throwing in complications, revelations, and side trips that constantly force your characters to change their plans keeps the audience intrigued and can make your script a literal "page-turner."

By definition, movies *move*. The speed at which your story develops can be key to how it is received. Being constantly aware of your script's pacing and employing the remedies suggested above to address pacing problems can go a long way toward keeping your audiences' asses from squirming and keeping them planted firmly on the edge of their seats — right where they belong.

OFF TO SEE THE WIZARD
Why the First Plot Point Comes Sooner Than You Think

Ever since the 1979 publication of Syd Field's seminal how-to book, *Screenwriting*, the concept of the Three Act Structure has become an accepted maxim among Hollywood filmmakers. The paradigm, which divides a screen story into Act One (30 pages), Act Two (60 pages), and Act Three (30 pages), has helped hundreds of writers, producers, and directors better structure and pace their cinematic scenarios. But at the same time, a strict adherence to the model has caused many filmmakers, particularly novice writers, problems when it comes to pacing their screenplay's early passages. As a result, many spec screenplays tend to be very lethargic in their first thirty pages, with the writer holding back any meaningful action until Act Two. This is a deadly — yet easily avoidable — mistake.

When discussing the Three Act Structure, most people make reference to two principal "Plot Points," key events which spin the story's course in some unexpected direction. Theoretically, the first plot point occurs right around page 30, and serves as the dividing point between Act One and Act Two. The second plot point occurs roughly around page 90 and separates the second and third acts.

Although one can convincingly argue that first acts generally are roughly one quarter of a film's total running time, it is a mistake to believe that the first plot point and the end of Act One are one and the same. They aren't. In fact, the first plot point often occurs as early as ten pages/minutes before the story moves into Act Two. Understanding this difference can help make your screenplay swifter, stronger, and more interesting.

Before we get into specific examples, let's define our terms. By "plot points," we mean a significant event that shakes up a character's life and causes him or her to make a whole new set of decisions. Often it's nothing more than the presentation of the "problem" that the hero will spend the rest of the movie trying to solve. A plot point is often sudden and unexpected: a gunshot, a blow to the head, a serving of divorce papers, receiving an eviction notice, being blown back in time. On the other hand, the point of demarcation between dramatic acts we'll call the "Act Curtain." This is an obvious reference to the physical curtain used in stageplays to separate one act from the next. Although no literal "curtain" is used in films, act curtains can usually be identified by the use of optical devices such as lapse dissolves, fade outs, wipes, or jump cuts that transport us across vast distances in time and space.

A great example of the difference between plot points and act curtains can be found in the 1939 classic *The Wizard of Oz*. Most of us became familiar with the movie via television, which has obvious act curtains — in the form of commercial breaks. Here their placement can be particularly instructive.

The Wizard of Oz contains what is probably the most obvious — and visual — plot point in the history of cinema, that being the moment Dorothy steps through her farmhouse door into Munchkinland, and the film shifts from black and white to Technicolor. It's at that point that all of Dorothy's plans and expectations change. She realizes, as she so aptly tells her dog, Toto: "I have a feeling we're not in Kansas anymore." But is this the end of Act One? No. In fact, we're only about twenty minutes into the film. We still have the entire Munchkinland scene to go through, climaxed by Good Witch Glinda's command for Dorothy to "Follow the Yellow Brick Road." Now Dorothy not only has a problem — how to get home — but she also has a plan: to see the fabled Wizard. And what happens to us TV watchers as she and Toto go off skipping off to see the Wizard? Commercial! Yes, every time the movie was shown on TV, this was the first commercial break. Why? Because whether the programmers knew it or not, this is in fact the end of Act One. And, not coincidentally, it's also the thirty-minute mark. Long before the modern screenplay gurus, those execs at MGM knew all about story structure.

Now lets jump ahead to 1985 and that Academy Award-nominated Robert Zemekis/Bob Gale sci-fi favorite, *Back to the Future*.

Here again, the first plot point and the Act One curtain are several minutes apart. The Act One plot point is obvious: it's the moment when Marty McFly accidentally takes his time-traveling DeLorean from 1985 back to 1955. This established his problem. But that's not the end of Act One. No, first he has to crash land in the farmer's barn, get mistaken for an invading alien, speed away amidst a hail of buckshot, and drive to the Lyon Estates Subdivision — only to discover that his home hasn't even been built yet! He then parks the DeLorean behind the Lyon Estates billboard and heads off on foot to find a way "back to the future." It's the modern equivalent of Dorothy dancing off down the Yellow Brick Road. (And indeed, Marty *is* "Off to See the Wizard" — in this case, Doc Brown!) And how do we know we've moved to Act Two? Because, in a jarring jump cut, night turns to day; the dark, brooding chords of Alan Sylvestri's score change into the giddy strains of "Mr. Sandman" — and Marty McFly has jumped from being miles outside Hill Valley to being smack in the town square. This abrupt shift in time, space, and mood is a sure indication that we're in the next act.

Finally, let's look at one of the ultimate popcorn movies, 1998's *Armageddon* (written by just about every scribe in Hollywood). The first act plot point — that is, the presentation of the problem — comes very early in the film: NASA scientists discover that an asteroid "the size of Texas" is about to slam into the earth and ruin everybody's day. The rest of Act One is devoted to figuring out show to solve the problem, which ultimately involves assembling Bruce Willis and his team of oil-drilling misfits to help plant a nuke at the asteroid's core. Although the first plot point comes very early in the picture, Act One itself isn't over until Willis and friends agree to save the world. Then, once again, we're "Off to See the Wizard," in this case a space rock with a bad attitude.

There are hundreds of similar examples to raise, but brevity, as the Bard himself wrote, is the soul of wit. Suffice it to say that the best examples of modern screenwriting suggest that the first act plot point — the moment when the hero's problem appears and his or her life changes — does not occur at page 30, but more often at some point between pages 20 and 25 (in a standard 120-page screenplay). The hero must then react to this event and formulate a new course of action. When he or she embarks on this new course, generally around page 30, *this* is the end of Act One. And it's usually denoted by a "curtain" in the form of an abrupt shift in time, space, and/or mood.

Understanding and utilizing this fundamental difference between the first act plot point and the Act One curtain can help you speed your script along and pace your key dramatic beats in places that best serve your story, and your audience.

MECHANICS

MORE THAN MEETS THE EYE
The Importance of Escalation in Dramatic Storytelling

"The plot thickens" may be a literary cliché, but the idea of a narrative that suddenly becomes increasingly complex is — and always will be — a key to effective storytelling. Danger that grows over time, threats that loom larger with every scene, and stakes that suddenly rise precipitously invariably engage and hold an audience's attention. By contrast, a story that lays out its objectives and consequences early on and then offers no subsequent surprises must work twice as hard to maintain an audience's interest.

How often have you found yourself watching a movie and, about halfway through it...had the uncomfortable feeling that, while there may be frenetic action on the screen, nothing was actually *happening*? There's a good chance that a lack of narrative escalation was the culprit. What do we mean when we talk about narrative "escalation"? Merriam-Webster defines "escalation" as, "to increase in extent, volume, number, amount, intensity, or scope." In other words, as a dramatic storyline develops, it constantly needs *more*: more enemies, nastier threats, greater consequences. Whether they be dramas or comedies, stories work best when, partway through the story, the hero suddenly realizes that he or she is up against a whole lot more than originally bargained for. Hollywood's filmography is crammed with stories that employ escalation to great effect. For example:

Mr. Smith Goes to Washington (1939) — Early in the story, Junior Senator Jefferson Smith introduces a seemingly innocuous bill to establish a boys' camp (low stakes); by Act Three, he's fighting for his political life (high stakes).

On the Waterfront (1954) — Terry Malloy dreams of being a prize-fighter (low stakes), witnesses a murder (higher stakes) and must then take a stand against an entire mob-run labor union (highest stakes).

The Sound of Music (1965) — Sister Maria is assigned to look after a widowed Austrian naval officer's seven children (low stakes); by Act Three, she's helping the entire family flee Nazi tyranny (high stakes).

Taxi Driver (1975) — An emotionally conflicted Manhattan cab driver befriends a twelve-year-old prostitute (low stakes) and eventually becomes a would-be presidential assassin and vigilante (high stakes).

Home Alone (1990) — A second grader must deal with having been accidentally abandoned by his family (low stakes) and then outsmart the two burglars who want to pick the house clean (high stakes).

Pirates of the Caribbean: The Curse of the Black Pearl (2003) — Blacksmith Will Turner pines for the daughter of the royal governor (low stakes), only to eventually find himself battling an entire boatload of "undead" buccaneers (high stakes).

In all of these successful films (and in countless others), the filmmakers engage our hearts and mind by periodically *upping the stakes*. The tornadoes get larger (*Twister*). The waves get taller (*The Perfect Storm*). The damage becomes greater (*Meet the Parents*).

Escalation keeps us guessing. It keeps us off balance. It helps avoid that dreaded problem, "predictability." Which is not to say that you can't write an effective movie that doesn't include escalating danger. There are many successful films — some of them very successful — that lay all their cards on the table within the first thirty minutes and then go no further. For example:

Jaws (1975) — There's a big shark at the beginning of the film, and the same big shark at the end of the film.

Jurassic Park (1993) — Killer dinosaurs are let loose at the end of Act One. In Act Three, they're still on the loose.

Maid in Manhattan (2002) — A debonair politician falls for a seemingly high-class woman who's really a lowly hotel maid. And that's about it.

Since these kinds of stories don't noticeably escalate, the only way for the filmmakers to maintain interest is to cram the story with action (as in *Jaws*), effective set-pieces (as in *Jurassic* Park), or with frequent plots twists (as in *Maid in Manhattan*). (Note that a "plot twist" is *not* escalation. A "twist" is simply an unexpected turn of events. It doesn't mean that the stakes have gotten any larger. For example, in the aforementioned *Maid in Manhattan*, the obligatory end-of-Act Two "twist" is that the rich politician, played by Ralph Fiennes, discovers that Jennifer Lopez is not the woman she's pretending to be. It may send the story moving in a new direction, but it doesn't make the conflict any "larger.") Such techniques can work, but they require significantly more creative energy on the writer's part and, more often than not, fail to pay off.

Here then are some guidelines to help you use the element of "escalation" effectively in *your* screenplays:

Have your hero make a "discovery" near that midpoint that reveals a "larger" conflict than was originally anticipated. A classic example of this is the prototypical James Bond film, *Goldfinger*. That film begins with 007 investigating millionaire industrialist Auric Goldfinger for international gold smuggling; at the mid-point, Bond is not only captured, but he discovers that Goldfinger is planning to increase the value of his gold hoard by blowing up Fort Knox with an atomic bomb!

Increasingly widen the physical scope of your story. In the thriller *Se7en*, the early scenes all take place in dark, claustrophobic interiors. The story then becomes larger and larger until the final sequence, which is set out in the vast and blindingly bright desert area surrounding Palm Springs. The Master of Suspense, Alfred Hitchcock frequently "widened" his physical scope as his films progressed. For example, *North by Northwest* begins in the comfortable confines of Manhattan, then moves cross country until it climaxes with an improbable chase on the face of Mount Rushmore.

Slowly direct personal danger toward your hero. Many movies begin with the hero standing outside the actual danger zone. By the third act, he or she is directly in the line of fire. For example, 1991's *Silence of the Lambs* begins with FBI rookie Special Agent Clarice Starling merely being asked to interrogate imprisoned serial killer Hannibal Lector. By the third act climax, Starling is single-handedly taking on the serial killer dubbed "Buffalo Bill." This technique is also used in the aforementioned *Jaws*. Although the actual danger in the movie never changes, it's the fact that Sheriff Brody eventually goes out to track and confront the killer shark *himself* that makes the movie increasingly interesting.

Increase the level of physical activity. One of Hollywood's oldest escalation techniques is to end the movie with a big chase scene. It worked in the days of Buster Keaton, and it works just as well in the days of Jerry Bruckheimer.

Change your character's motives to embrace "deeper" goals. This involves employing emotional rather than physical escalation. For example, in 1988's *Rain Man*, Tom Cruise's Charlie Babbit is initially interested only in making money. By the end of the story, he's fighting for custody of his autistic older brother. The animated modern classic *Shrek* begins with the hero wanting nothing more than to rid his home of interlopers; towards the end of Act Two, it turns into a love story.

Increase overall emotional complexity. Actions have consequences, and the more difficult these consequences are to deal with, the more compelling your story can be. A good case-in-point is 2003's *Mystic River*. It's bad enough that the lead character, played by Sean Penn, must deal with the brutal murder of his teenage daughter. He must then face the possibility that the killer is his emotionally troubled childhood friend (Tim Robbins) and then the realization that, in his desire to exact justice, he has killed the wrong man. What began as a simple revenge story eventually becomes much, much more.

Escalation keeps the story moving. It keeps the narrative interesting. It keeps the audience involved. Employ one or more of the techniques described above to give your screenplay power and scope, your characters extra depth and dimension. Good stories are always about growth, and a great way to get a character to grow is to have their story grow around them.

Escalation is more than gimmick. It is the essence of good storytelling.

HARD TARGET
Keeping Your Hero in the Center of the Action

In the 1999 thriller *8MM*, Nicolas Cage played a private eye who's hired to investigate the apparent murder of a young woman in a "snuff" film. The movie (screenplay by Andrew Kevin Walker) covered much the same territory as Paul Schrader's 1979 drama *Hardcore*, in which George C. Scott played a man desperate to find his daughter, who's disappeared into the porno underworld. Despite its age, *Hardcore* remains the more effective of the two movies for one simple reason: Scott's character is seeking something personal, whereas Cage's P.I. is merely doing a job. Yes, Cage's character is emotionally ravaged by his investigation, but the fact remains that he can walk away from danger at any time with little or no personal consequence. And having such an "easy out" always makes for poor screen drama — a situation that no doubt contributed to that film's poor showing at the box office.

Since the days of Sophocles, the best dramatic stories have usually involved characters who are pressured into taking a difficult course of action. When writing a screen story — be it drama or comedy — you want to put your hero in a situation that involves a large element of personal risk. Success must not only promise great rewards, but failure must also threaten severe personal consequences. In short, you want to push your hero into a corner from which there is no escape. There are several proven ways to put your hero in the center of the action, to keep both him and the audience interested in seeing the story out to the bitter end.

Put your hero in personal jeopardy. Putting your hero's life, fortune, or reputation directly on the line is the simplest and often the most effective way to create dramatic pressure. For example, in James Cameron's megahit *Titanic*, Jack Dawson and Rose DeWitt Bukater have to find a way off the sinking ship or they die. There's no more direct jeopardy that that. Or perhaps there is. In the *Lord of the Rings* trilogy, the hobbit Frodo *must* destroy the "one ring" or evil will engulf the world — forever. Of course, the consequences may not be global. In 1998's *A Simple Plan* (screenplay by Scott B. Smith, adapted from his novel), brothers Hank and Jacob Mitchell have to find a way to conceal their discovery of $4.4 million or lose the money, possibly go to jail, and even lose their lives. None of these people can simply walk away from the challenges before them.

Put the life of someone the hero cares about in jeopardy. Although direct personal jeopardy is the easiest kind of pressure to identify with, true heroism usually requires a character to put his or her life on the line for someone else. This is why cops, doctors, lawyers, and detectives always make solid dramatic heroes: their jobs require them to work on behalf of other people. However, in movies — as opposed to episodic television — it's usually not enough for the "professional hero" to merely do his or her job. The "client" needs to mean something to the hero personally; otherwise there's no compelling reason to take enormous risks. (Money alone is rarely sufficient. Morally speaking, it's the lowest of all motivation forces.)

For example, in the seminal action film *Die Hard*, it wasn't enough for Detective John McClane to be trapped in a high-rise office building overrun by terrorists. No, his estranged wife needed to be among the terrorist's prisoners. When Jackie Chan's Inspector Lee came to Los Angeles in 1998's *Rush Hour*, it wasn't just to rescue a kidnapped girl; it was to rescue the kidnapped daughter of a close friend. And while Warrant Officer Ripley may spend much of James Cameron's 1986 *Aliens* trying to save her own neck, it's her unwavering defense of the orphan Newt — a girl who has become her surrogate daughter — that truly turns this character into an action hero.

Put your hero in an ethical quandary. Some stories don't put their heroes or someone the hero loves in direct jeopardy, but instead force their protagonists to fight for a concept or an idea. For example, in 1998's *A Civil Action*, attorney Jan Schlichtmann is at first motivated by money, but later loses everything because of an overwhelming need to see justice served. In 1998's *Saving Private Ryan*, Captain Miller may start out doing nothing more than reluctantly following orders, but he's ultimately driven by the belief that by saving one man, he can in essence save countless others. (This was the same theme Spielberg explored in 1993's *Schindler's List*.) Even incorrigible Billy Bob Thornton sacrifices possible escape to satisfy a dim-witted child's Christmas wish in the otherwise delightfully crass and cynical 2003 black comedy *Bad Santa*.

Done properly, fighting for a cause can be just as personal as fighting to save one's own life. The trick is to create a character whose sense of self is part and parcel of the cause for which he or she is fighting. You want to create a situation where your character must fight for a cause, or lose all self-respect and sense of self worth. Very often, heroes won't even know they have such moral depth until they're forced by circumstances to make an ethical decision. (This was certainly the case with both Oskar Schindler and Jan Schlichtmann, both based on real-life heroes.) This revelation then becomes a key component of the character's arc.

Regardless of which tack you choose, you always want to consciously keep your hero in the center of the action. Never create a set of circumstances from which your hero can simply walk away and lose nothing of importance. Do so and you risk having your audience walk away — regardless of your hero's ultimate decision.

A (SET) PIECE-OF-THE-ACTION
Why No One Buys an Action Film for Its Plot

Action is a Hollywood staple. Since the dawn of cinema itself, few genres have been able to draw large audiences more reliably than good old-fashioned chase-'em-down-and-shoot-'em-ups. Whether it's John Wayne trying to seize control of a runaway stagecoach or Gene Hackman trying to outrace a hijacked subway train or James Bond duking it out with a seven-foot-tall assassin, movies have always been particularly adept at wowing ticket-buyers with fast-paced, visually stunning sequences of physical derring-do. In fact, it can be argued that action is the one thing movies do better than any other medium. Which may be why they're called *movies*.

Of course, today's audiences are more sophisticated than they were fifty or even twenty years ago, and filmmaking technology has grown equally sophisticated to help meet the demands of today's been-there-done-that moviegoers. But without innovative ideas to drive that technology, all those million-dollar Steadicams and flying wires are just super-expensive paperweights. Even in this world of micro-cameras and virtual stuntmen, it all still begins with the written word.

What are the secrets of writing a great action script? Well, like all screenplays, action scripts need to begin with an intriguing premise, then expand upon that premise with a story filled with escalating jeopardy and populated by empathetic characters who say and do interesting things in interesting ways, all leading up to a thrilling climax and satisfactory conclusion. However, what tends to distinguish action scripts from those of other genres is their dependence on set-pieces. One can even argue that action scripts don't really need intriguing premises, complex stories, empathetic characters, or good dialogue — *especially* not good dialogue — if their set-pieces are sufficiently original and exciting. The combined filmographies of John Wayne, Charles Bronson, Chuck Norris, Steven Seagal, and Keanu Reeves stand as ample evidence that an actor need not be Laurence Olivier to enjoy a long and lucrative film career — as long as he is placed in the center of frenetic and creatively staged action scenes that make audiences gasp, laugh, and cheer at their sheer audacity.

What exactly *is* a "set-piece"? In Hollywood terms, a set-piece is a single, often elongated scene that is restricted to a single location or set of related locations and involves a character attempting to solve a single problem while every conceivable obstacle is thrown in his or her way. It's a "mini-movie" with a clear beginning, middle, and end that often has only a minimal — if any — impact on the actual course of the larger story.

Some of filmdom's most famous action set-pieces include:
- The chase across the ice flow in *Uncle Tom's Cabin* (various silent versions)
- The chariot race from *Ben-Hur* (both the 1925 and 1959 versions)
- James Bond battling Odd Job in the vault of Fort Knox in *Goldfinger*
- The runaway subway chase in *The French Connection*
- The truck chase from *Raider's of the Lost Ark*
- John McClane's rooftop escape in the original *Die Hard*
- The first T-Rex battle in *Jurassic Park*
- Neo and Agent Smith's subway station battle in *The Matrix*
- Legolas single-handedly taking down a giant war elephant in *Lord of the Rings: The Return of the King*
- Almost all of *Troy*

Very often, a set-piece involves a character doing nothing more than getting into trouble and then getting out of it. Maybe the character comes away with a tidbit of information that helps move the story forward. Maybe not. Only if the set-piece occurs at the movie's climax will the outcome have a serious impact on the story's course, that outcome usually being the defeat or death of the villain.

If so little actually *happens* during an action set-piece, why are they so interesting? As stated above, set-pieces succeed when the writer, director, and stunt-coordinator work together to throw every conceivable obstacle into the character's path as he or she struggles to move from Point A to Point B — or even from Point A to Point B and back to Point A again. To wax poetic, it is the journey, not the destination that is important.

Assuming you already have the bare bones of an action story in place — premise, characters, storyline, etc. — here are some ways to conceive and develop action set-pieces that will raise your screenplay from the ordinary to the extraordinary.

Choose your battlefields wisely. Action scenes — and by this we generally mean *fight* scenes — can be made particularly memorable simply by the choice of location. A fist-fight in a parking lot is mundane. The same fist-fight on a rooftop is automatically more interesting. A fist-fight on the wing of a moving airplane is *very* interesting. The writers who worked for Alfred Hitchcock were famous for finding famous and exotic locations (the Statue of Liberty, Mount Rushmore, etc.) for their chases and fight sequences. For four decades the James Bond films have exploited the world's most exotic destinations to bring us weird and wonderful arenas for fights that continuously pushed the envelope of plausibility. Technology — from the whirling rides of an amusement park to the industrial robots of a modern auto assembly plant — offers particularly good backdrops for memorable action sequences.

Exploit the environment. After deciding on the "arena" — be it literal or figurative — for your action scene, make the setting itself a major factor in the scene's development. Turn the environment's physical aspects into obstacles for your hero to overcome, and transform props into weapons of both offense and defense. Exploitable elements can be obvious (the spinning blades in a sawmill) or they can be subtle (cutlery at a fancy dinner party). Jackie Chan is a master of this technique, having turned such mundane props as library books, ladders, and shopping carts into amazing action props. Of course, coming up with such "gags" (as they're known in "The Biz") requires an advanced visual imagination. But then, that's why you're writing movies and not technical manuals, right?

Play double jeopardy. The more danger your characters are in, the more exciting your action scene is going to be. Which is why many great action scenes involve multiple levels of danger. Remember the fight-at-the-Flying-Wing sequence in *Raiders of the Lost Ark*? Poor Indiana Jones had to battle a huge bare-chested Nazi hand-to-hand while simultaneously dodging spinning propellers on a runaway airplane, machine gun fire, burning oil, exploding fuel tanks, and truckloads of German infantry. Talk about a tough day at the office! This same drive for double- or even triple-jeopardy is why we so often see fight scenes on moving train cars (watch out for the low bridge!), on open skyscraper skeletons, and in other locations where the environment is just as deadly as the adversary himself. When writing an action scene, see how many simultaneous threats you can throw at *your* hero — then throw in one or two more just for fun.

Let your hero be constructive as well as destructive. A classic way to "spin" a fight scene or gun battle is to require your hero to protect or save something, while trying to defeat the bad guy. Sometimes this means the hero is protecting someone while trying to kill someone else, or it can involve trying to protect an inanimate object. (Both *Rush Hour* and *Shanghai Knights* used museum scenes where Jackie Chan struggled to protect priceless historical items while simultaneously knocking the crap out of the bad guys.) Requiring your hero to protect someone or something of value not only puts a great spin on what could otherwise be an ordinary action scene, but it serves to make the character more sympathetic.

Put your hero at a disadvantage. The greater the odds against your hero, the more interesting your set-piece will inevitably be. There are three ways to achieve this: (1) Give your antagonist superior capabilities, (2) Force your hero to fight multiple opponents, or (3) Disable your hero prior to the contest. Naturally, your set-piece can involve one or more of these techniques in any number of combinations. For example, *Pirates of the Caribbean: The Curse of the Black Pearl*, hero Orlando Bloom finds himself pitted against an entire phalanx of bloodthirsty pirates (option 2), but bloodthirsty pirates who also happen to be incapable of being killed (option 1). In the climax of the Oscar-winning *Gladiator*, General Maximus is put at a decided disadvantage when he's pitted against the well-trained Emperor Commodus (option 1) while at the same time suffering from a near-fatal stab wound (option 3).

Feel free to mix-and-match at your leisure.

Provide a punchline. Like a good joke, a good set-piece needs a good punchline. Sometimes it can just be something *huge* happening (a bridge collapses, a truck explodes, etc.) while the hero escapes, and sometimes it can literally be a joke. (A priceless vase that has somehow remained standing during the whole fight...shatters just as the hero finally dispatches the last of the bad guys.) The thing to remember is not to let your set-piece just *stop*. It needs a button. A curtain. Something that tells the audience, "It's over," and lets everyone catch their collective breath.

As long as there are motion pictures, there will be action films. How successful those films are will depend, in large part, not on the advances made by technology, but on the creativity and resourcefulness of those of us who begin with nothing but an idea and then shape and mold that idea into a screenplay. With sufficient skill, wit, and determination not to tread over old ground, we can make sure then when a director calls "Action!" — no one will be disappointed.

THE LAST LAUGH
The Best Way to Get Your Hands on Funny Money

There's nothing more transcendent than sitting at the back of a packed theater and listening to an audience howl with laughter at a comedy you've written. And there's nothing more painful than listening to that same audience respond with deadly silence to a joke you were certain would be a gutbuster.

What differentiates a successful comedy from a stinker? A million dollar comedy spec from a hundred pages of scratch paper? Although one could easily write an entire book on this topic — and many have tried — here are ten simple rules that will help you fashion your comedic idea into a screenplay that will have all of Hollywood laughing with you, and not at you:

Begin with a strong comedic premise. Most successful comedies are based on funny ideas. And what makes them funny is a sense of *irony*. For example, in *Liar, Liar*, it wasn't enough that a man was forced to tell the truth for twenty-four hours, it was that a *lawyer* — a professional prevaricator — was forced to do so. In *Analyze This*, screenwriters Peter Tolan, Harold Ramis, and Ken Lonergan didn't just send a man to a psychiatrist; they sent a *top mobster*, a man whose whole life has revolved around keeping secrets. Start with a strong *ironic* premise, and you're already halfway home.

Spin your premise in as many directions as possible. To best exploit your premise, you need to take your story places the audience isn't expecting. *Ruthless People*, *Groundhog Day*, and *Shakespeare in Love* are all examples of comedies that begin with simple premises and then repeatedly *twist* those premises to keep the humor fresh and unpredictable.

Decide who's funny — your hero or your universe. The best comedies tend to be those in which a wild, funny character is let loose in an otherwise sane world (*Ace Ventura, Legally Blonde, Elf, School of Rock*, etc.) or in which an ostensibly rational person is tested by what appears to be an insane universe (*Father of the Bride, After Hours*, the National Lampoon *Vacation* movies). When you try to make *everyone* funny, the results are usually far less than the sum of the parts.

Don't write for a specific actor or actress. Although a role may eventually be tailored for the talents of a Jim Carrey, an Adam Sandler, or a Reese Witherspoon, you should never write a part for any *specific* individual. After all, if that person is already a proven box office draw, chances are he or she is unavailable, too expensive, or so inundated with scripts that your particular project has only one chance in a million of getting noticed. Your chances will be far better if you write a character that can be played by any number of A-List performers.

Keep your tone consistent. Although every movie takes place in its own universe, comedies are particularly dependent on establishing rules of behavior — both physical and human — and then sticking to them. For example, if you're writing a smart, sophisticated comedy like *As Good As It Gets* or *Rushmore*, you don't want to undercut it with the kind of broad, crude slapstick found in movies like *American Pie* or *Bruce Almighty*. Conversely, if you're writing a live-action cartoon like *Inspector Gadget* or *Scooby-Doo*, it does you no good to toss in obtuse Woody Allen-isms or serious reflections on the human condition. "Funny" is usually dependent on context, and you have to ground your jokes in a foundation that remains solid and consistent throughout your story.

Focus on your set-pieces. It's often been said that for a comedy to sell, it needs at least five *big* laughs. And truly big laughs rarely arise from one-liners or stand-alone sight-gags, but from *set-pieces*, scenes that begin with a specific comic premise and then build and build toward a huge pay-off. For example, 1998's *There's Something About Mary* may have dragged in parts, but its key set-pieces — Matt Dillon trying to revive the "dead" dog, Ben Stiller and his "hair gel," etc. — produced such huge, sustained laughs that any faults the movie may have had were quickly forgiven.

Don't push too hard. A big mistake most novice comedy writers make is to try to make *everything* funny. Every character has to be wild and crazy. Every snippet of dialogue has to contain a wisecrack. The result of such comic overkill is usually a script that's mentally exhausting, if not downright unreadable. Remember, if everything's funny, then nothing's funny. It's far better to have a few strong, well-placed gags that produce big laughs than a relentless barrage of sight-gags and one-liners that result in nothing but tedium.

Ground your humor in truth. The most common criticism leveled against bad comedies is that they're "stupid." And what makes a comedy "stupid" is usually a simple lack of reality. At its most basic level, humor results from an exaggeration of simple human behavior. There must be a kernel of truth or logic in every joke, no matter how broad or grotesque, for it to produce a laugh. This is because laughter comes from *recognition*, and if we don't recognize something as being part of our own experience, there's no way we can find it funny. So never stray too far from the mundane world we all know and love in your search for big laughs.

Keep it short. Brevity really *is* the soul of wit. This is why most successful comedy screenplays come in at between ninety and 110 pages, versus 110-135 for action and dramatic scripts. It's just too hard — *physically* hard — to keep audiences laughing for more than ninety minutes straight, so it's best not to try.

End with a laugh. Just as all jokes end with a punchline, a good comedy screenplay will end with a strong laugh. This can be a joke, a sight-gag, a funny character reaction, or any other device that drop-kicks your story into the closing credits.

And now the final rule: *There Are No Rules.* Anything that produces a laugh, no matter how much it may violate the codified rules of comedy writing, is, by definition, funny. So never feel too constricted by rules and regulations when writing a comedy screenplay. Break the right rule at the right time and you could end up laughing all the way to the bank.

TALK IS CHEAP
Why Action Speaks Louder Than Words

Novice screenwriters often forget that the cinema is, above all, a *visual* medium. Because writers spend so much time dealing in words, it's easy to forget that, for its first twenty-five years, the motion picture industry produced a wholly silent product. With the exception of the occasional title card, stories were told solely through action, expression, and the juxtaposition of selected images. In fact, during the silent era, screenplays as we know them didn't even exist. Writers created "scenarios" — essentially a series of related events that, when edited together, became a recognizable story with a beginning, middle, and an end.

Not only were filmmakers able to mold classic comedies from "moving pictures," but also sprawling historical epics. Even the works of William Shakespeare managed to enthrall audiences worldwide without the benefit of a single spoken word.

Today, with sound such an integral part of the motion picture experience, screenwriters tend to forget how powerful imagery can be, not only in making a strong emotional impression, but also in communicating information essential to understanding a story or getting to know a character. In fact, there are so many screenplays with an emphasis on dialogue and *explaining* things that one has to wonder why the authors chose to write movies at all — instead of word-heavy novels or talky stageplays.

When designing your screenplay, pay as much attention as possible to the *visual* aspects of your story. This doesn't mean description, setting, or special effects, but *actions* and *behaviors* that move your story forward.

For example, in the 2000 New Line picture *Frequency* (screenplay by Toby Emmerich), Dennis Quaid's character is a heroic firefighter with a penchant for taking crazy risks. A bad writer might stage the introductory scene in the fire station. After coming back from a call, the Quaid character would be called into the captain's office where he'd be chewed out for being a "hot-dogger," putting his and other people's lives in danger, etc. Fortunately, Toby Emmerich is not a bad writer. He introduces Quaid's character by actually showing him risk life and limb to rescue some city workers trapped in a sewer directly beneath a burning overturned fuel truck about to explode. The sequence is riveting. It's visual. And it tells us what we need to know about this character without the specifics being spelled out for us. We can *see for ourselves* what kind of a man he is.

As a screenwriter, you need to take a similar tack. Is your character a great lawyer? Then *show* him or her performing a stunning cross-examination in a courtroom. Is he an awkward teenager? Then show him tongue-tied when he tries to ask a beautiful girl out on a date. Is she a devoted mother? Then *show* her racing through a thunderstorm to bring her little girl the all-important school project she forgot at home. *Show*, don't tell.

Key events in your story must also find their way *visually* into your movie. Which do you think will have more impact — a police captain announcing, "We just picked up the suspect," or actually *showing* cops surrounding a building, busting down a door, then chasing a fleeing suspect before finally placing him in custody? Which carries more weight — a girl telling her date, "You're a great dancer," or a fully choreographed scene in which the couple set the dance floor aflame? Which do you suppose will make it into your movie's trailer — a frenzied reporter bursting into a newsroom to announce "A giant spaceship has just crashed into the Hollywood Bowl!" or a scene in which a giant spaceship *actually crashes* into the Hollywood Bowl? The answers are obvious. *Show*, don't tell. Finally, keep in mind that one picture is, indeed, worth a thousand words. As a result, it's often not necessary to explain *how* someone has made a discovery or reached a conclusion as long as the elements necessary to arrive at this point are visually present.

Star Wars, for example, is rife with short, visually rich scenes that require only one or two lines of dialogue to move the story forward.

When Darth Vader's forces are on the desert planet Tatooine in search of C3PO and R2D2, there's a wonderfully economical scene in which a stormtrooper, examining the area around the crashed escape pod, stands up holding a ring-like bit of metal and says to his partner, "Look, sir — 'droids!" End of scene. There's no discussion of where the metal part came from, what it signifies, or what the stormtroopers are going to do about it. There doesn't have to be. We know the bad guys are in hot pursuit and it will just be a matter of time before the robots are located. Likewise, when the evil Darth Vader commences his interrogation of Princess Leia, he doesn't even bother to introduce the floating "torture 'droid" that accompanies him. There's no need to explain the contraption or frighten the prisoner with horrific descriptions of what lies ahead. Just one look at the sinister orb with its nasty-looking appendages and foot-long hypodermic needle tells us that the brave princess is about to be in a world of pain. George Lucas may have lost his touch in his later years, but back in his prime, he knew it was always better to *show* rather than tell.

A singular exception to the "Show, Don't Tell" rule is courtroom testimony. Often, when creating a courtroom scene, novice writers will use flashbacks to visually portray the events relayed by a witness on the stand. While this approach is sometimes appropriate, it usually is more distracting than it is cinematic. This is because, in a courtroom scene, the focus is usually not so much the testimony itself, but the *emotional impact* of this testimony on the witness and/or the people being discussed. We need to stay in the here-and-now so we can watch trapped characters vent, squirm, and otherwise go through the emotional wringer. But, as stated above, the courtroom scene is the exception, not the rule, when it comes to exploiting the visual power of motion pictures. Whenever possible, *show* us what happens rather than telling us about it.

How far should you take this idea? Well, back in the mid-'80s, action star Sylvester Stallone said — perhaps facetiously — that the perfect motion picture script would contain only one line of dialogue. Just one line.

And no doubt, that line would have been "Yo."

SPIN CITY
Giving Familiar Scenes an Original "Kick"

All writers want their work to be fresh. New. Original. Unique. Ideally, every scene we create, every line of dialogue we write, will read like nothing that has ever been written before. In the best of all possible worlds, the end result of our groundbreaking creativity will send readers, producers, and studios executives leaping out of their chairs with excitement — and reaching for their checkbooks in a mad dash to secure for themselves a story that stands alone.

Unfortunately, things rarely work out that way.

Despite our most noble creative urges, most stories demand scenes and scenarios that are, in one way or another, familiar. Anyone writing in a genre — be it police procedural, action, legal thriller, western, medical drama, horror, romantic comedy, etc. — knows that certain kinds of scenes are virtually unavoidable. The briefing scene. The interrogation scene. The chase scene. The love scene. The shoot-out. The courtroom scene. The "girls do lunch" scene. These kinds of scenes are not only part and parcel of genre pictures, they virtually define them.

Good screenwriting then often depends not on devising scenes and sequences that are wholly original, but in finding new ways to present them. It's about putting a new "spin" on a stock scene — to raise it above the realm of cliché — to give the familiar new life and new excitement. Here, then, are some strategies you can use to give even your stock (or obligatory) scenes an extra kick — and raise the bar on the product you produce:

Exposition: Traditionally, one of the dullest scenes in any movie is the "briefing" or exposition scene. This is the scene where the authority figure (police captain, commanding officer, senior law partner, professor, editor, etc.) tells the hero (cop, soldier, lawyer, student, writer, etc.) just what the problem is and what he or she is going to have to do about it. Usually this scene takes place in an office setting with the characters trading dialogue back and forth — perhaps using maps, photos, etc. as visual support.

There are many ways to make such pedestrian yet essential scenes "come alive" on screen. For example, use an unusual setting. Since such a scene traditionally involves an authority figure, come up with a setting that reflects that character's position or personality and gives the scene some flair. For example, an exchange between a police officer and his or her superior could take place on a firing range, in a gym, backstage at a TV studio, on the captain's cabin cruiser or at a baseball game. Dangerous locations — like under-construction high-rises, scrap yards, or factories — provide natural physical tension for long dialogue scenes. You can also conduct your exposition over physical action, such as a chase scene, or just an extended bit of physical business involving one or both of the characters. Or you can layer your scene with obstacles. For example, a dozen other things could be going on that demand the authority figure's attention while he or she is trying to brief the hero. You could set the scene outdoors and make violent weather a factor. Or perhaps there's remodeling going on next door causing all kinds of awful noises that interfere with the natural flow of conversation. (In *The Matrix*, the Wachowski Brothers spiced up a simple dressing down scene between Thomas "Neo" Anderson and his corporate boss by placing a window washer directly outside the office. The constant squeaking of the washer's squeegee — sounding like nails on a blackboard — gave the scene an extra and very effective edge.)

Chase scenes: Chase scenes can be dressed up in three basic ways. The first is to come up with an unusual mode of transportation combination. Car vs. car is hackneyed, which is why filmmakers have tried combinations ranging from car vs. train (according to Hollywood legend, the famous *French Connection* chase was originally going to be between two cars until screenwriter Ernest Tidyman was touring the location looking for inspiration and an elevated subway car thundered overhead. The rest was cinematic history) to car vs. helicopter (*The Italian Job*) to helicopter vs. motorcycle

MECHANICS

(*Tomorrow Never Dies*) to horse vs. truck (*Raiders of the Lost Ark*) to man vs. cropduster (*North by Northwest*). There have been helicopter chases (*Rambo*) and hovercraft chases (*Die Another Day*) and even bobsled chases (*On Her Majesty's Secret Service*). What unusual vehicles or combination of vehicles can you come up with? Car vs. Rollerblades? Ultra-light vs. Segway? The stranger the better.

The second way to goose your chase scene is to come up with unusual obstacles. The mom-with-a-baby-carriage gag was fresh when Tidyman did it in *The French Connection*, but now obstacles need to be bigger, stranger, and even more surprising. (Or you can parody old gags, as Graham Yost did in 1994's *Speed* when he put empty cans in a baby carriage that gets broadsided by the runaway bus.)

The third strategy is to layer your chase scene with multiple lines of action. Instead of having one guy chasing another guy, have one guy chasing a second guy chasing a third guy who's chasing the first guy. Or have one guy chasing another guy at the same time both are trying to escape from certain doom. (Watching Billy Zane trying to shoot Leonardo DiCaprio while the Titanic is sinking beneath the both of them is always amusing.)

Love scenes: The strategy for creating memorable love/sex scenes is no different than creating unusual chase and expository scenes. Look for unusual locations for your couple to get it on. (Anyplace but the bedroom.) Introduce obstacles that prevent the couple from enjoying quiet, conventional coitus. (Physical impediments, the danger of being caught, time pressure, etc.) And layer your love scenes with multiple lines of action (e.g. dialogue, movement of other characters, etc.) so as to accomplish multiple objectives simultaneously.

The danger, of course, is adding so much to a scene that it becomes "cluttered" and you lose focus. Which is why, when considering augmenting factors, you should choose those that grow naturally from the situation you've created and don't just appear out of proverbial left field.

Fortunately, it's easier to scale back than it is to expand, so it can't hurt to "pile it on" when writing otherwise mundane or generic sequences. Who knows, by refusing to settle for the familiar and plumbing your imagination for new and unique twists to clichéd scenes, you might just end up writing a classic.

THE BLACK MOMENT
Building to the Ultimate Cliffhanger

Earth has been laid waste by a ruthless alien civilization. A tiny band of survivors has launched one last, desperate counterattack. As a massive alien city-destroyer moves in to blast the last human outpost at Nevada's Area 51, Air Force F-18 Hornets stage a furious dogfight with a horde of alien fighters. Although the humans fight bravely, they're hopelessly out-numbered. The bottom of the saucer-like city-destroyer ominously opens, revealing its awesome energy weapon. The humans' Commanding General orders his troops to disable this weapon by any means, but the humans have no missiles left to fire. And then, one lone pilot — forgotten during the confusion of the battle — roars onto the scene brandishing a nuclear-tipped rocket. The pilot arms his weapon, locks his targeting computer on the energy projector, and fires. *But the missile locks malfunction! The missile won't release!*

This scene, from 1996's megahit *Independence Day*, written by Dean Devlin and Roland Emmerich, exemplifies a story-telling technique that all screenwriters should learn to master if they're going to create movies that deliver the greatest possible emotional punch. It involves taking your hero to the very edge of total disaster before allowing him to turn the tables and emerge triumphant. It means creating a specific moment when the audience — and perhaps even the hero himself — is convinced that all is indeed lost, that there's no way in hell this story is going to have a happy ending. Let us call this story beat the "Black Moment."

Recognizing the Black Moment: By definition, the Black Moment occurs in Act Three, your climax, when your hero and villain are locked in their last great battle. You've been building toward this moment since your first page: developing your hero's character, showing us how nasty your villain is, and establishing for your audience just what's at stake in the battle being waged. If you've designed your story correctly, your hero has entered this fight facing overwhelming odds. As the battle progresses, every gain has been offset by one or more losses. Finally, the hero is pushed into a corner — figuratively or perhaps even literally — from which there is seemingly no escape. The audience holds its collective breath. *How will the hero prevail?* This is the Black Moment. And it's delicious.

Why do we need Black Moments? Well, because movies just aren't very interesting without them. Victory that does not come easily is all the sweeter when it does finally arrive.

Black Moments in history: Just abut every great movie includes such a Black Moment. Here are some well-known examples:

E.T. The Extra-Terrestrial (screenplay by Melissa Mathison) — No, it's not E.T.'s "death." That comes too early in the story. It comes later, when the kids are racing E.T. through suburbia to his ship's forest landing site. After zig-zagging through various tract home neighborhoods with both the cops and FBI in hot pursuit, they turn a corner only to find the road blocked by the entire Spielbergville Police Force. Cops are in front of them. Cops are behind them. They're trapped with no way out...or *are* they? This is the Black Moment.

Titanic (screenplay by James Cameron) — The ship has sunk. So has Jack Dawson. Rose, minutes from becoming a human icicle, floats on a wooden headboard waiting to expire. Then she sees a light in the darkness. She hears a muffled voice call, "Is anyone alive?" She tries to yell out, but her voice is too weak. The most she can muster is a faint whisper. The lifeboat rows on, unaware of her presence just a few yards away. Rose begins to cry. She knows she's doomed. This is the Black Moment.

A Few Good Men (screenplay by Aaron Sorkin, based on his play) — Lieutenant Kaffe has crusty Colonel Jessup on the witness stand, but is unable to get him to admit that he ordered the Code Red hazing of an enlisted man under his command. If Kaffe can't get Jessup to confess, his own career will be ruined. *He'll* be prosecuted under the rules of military law. His one promising avenue of inquiry has

THE BLACK MOMENT just led nowhere; the judge prepares to dismiss Jessup from the witness stand. Jessup glares at the upstart lieutenant with murder in his eyes. Kaffe is looking at one big Black Moment.

The Lord of the Rings: The Return of the King (screenplay by Frances Walsh, Phillipa Boyens, and Peter Jackson), the climax finds hobbit Frodo standing on a precipice overlooking the molten core of Mount Doom. Having traveled hundreds of miles to destroy the One Ring in this magma stew, Frodo — weakened and exhausted — appears to finally succumb to the ring's power and places it on his finger. This terrifying turn is then compounded by the reappearance of the presumed-dead Gollum, who proceeds to literally bite the ring off of Frodo's hand and claim his "precious" for himself. The corrupted monster then dances with jubilation, his evil dream having at last been fulfilled. A classic Black Moment.

Secret weapons: Once you've written a Black Moment, the trick is to get out of it in a way that makes sense, that isn't a cheat. You accomplish this the same way a stage magician pulls off a seemingly impossible piece of prestidigitation: *preparation*. Usually, this involves setting up the key to your hero's salvation — a secret weapon, as it were, earlier in the story — then pulling it out at the last possible moment.

In *E.T.*, for example, Mathison earlier established that E.T. can make bicycles fly (the classic across-the-moon scene). So when the kids encounter the roadblock, what happens? E.T. sends *all* the bicycles leaping skyward, up and over the heads of the startled cops. It's fantastic, to be sure, but it's not a *cheat*: we saw E.T. do this same thing earlier. It's part of the movie's reality.

In *Titanic*, Rose saves herself by gathering her wits, swimming over to a dead ship's officer, and grabbing the whistle from around his neck; a whistle we saw him blow earlier. The people in the rescue boat hear the whistle, and Rose is saved.

In *A Few Good Men*, Kaffe is — at the last possible moment — able to find a logical flaw in Colonel Jessup's seemingly airtight cover story, a flaw that cuts straight to the heart of Jessup's self-image. Suddenly, the arrogant Colonel finds himself caught in a web of lies from which the only escape is to admit weakness. "I want the truth!," Kaffe demands. "You can't handle the truth!," Jessup bellows. But the truth *is* revealed, and we marvel at the elegance of Kaffe's reasoning.

In *The Lord of the Rings*, Frodo, having been forcibly freed from the ring's seductive influence, hurls himself at Gollum, sending the creature and the ring to their fiery doom.

Supporting characters to the rescue: Another way to get out of a Black Moment is to have a supporting character (one we've presumably forgotten about) come to the rescue. In *ID4*, the heroic F-18 pilot (played by Randy Quaid) is a secondary character at best. We also see this technique used in *Star Wars*, when Han Solo saves Luke Skywalker from Darth Vader. And in *Die Hard*, when Reginald VelJohnson saves Bruce Willis from Alexander Godunov in the movie's coda. And when Linda Fiorentino blasts the bug who's about to gobble up Will Smith at the climax of *Men in Black*. As with the "secret weapon" approach, *preparation* here is critical. The rescuer has to be someone we already know, and someone who has a legitimate reason for being on the scene; not just be a passerby who happens to be in the right place at the right time. Such rescues work best when they also demonstrate growth in the supporting character. In *Star Wars*, Han Solo was supposed to have run off with his reward, but instead demonstrates bravery by returning to the scene of the final battle. VelJohnson's cop was supposed to be phobic about firearms, but here manages to fire a gun to save a friend. And Fiorentino's character had been a classic damsel-in-distress until she picked up one of those chrome-plated sap rifles and became one of the boys.

A great third act climax is important to all screen stories, be they dramatic, comedic, or romantic. And to milk that climax for all it's worth, a Black Moment is essential. Put your hero in jeopardy, then make matters progressively worse for him. Push him into a corner and give him no visible way out. But plant the key to his triumph earlier in the story, so that when your hero pulls it out, the audience responds with a collective *a-ha!*

LASTING IMPRESSIONS
Finding the Means to Justify Your End

It's been said that people remember the first lines of novels — and the last lines of movies. Certainly such classic ending lines as "Tomorrow is another day" (*Gone with the Wind*), "I have the feeling this is the beginning of a beautiful friendship" (*Casablanca*), and "Forget it, Jake, it's Chinatown" (*Chinatown*) are today as firmly ensconced in our lexicon as "Call me Ishmael," "It was the best of times, it was the worst of times," and the immortal "It was a dark and stormy night."

The importance of a good ending cannot be overstated. How an audience feels the moment the lights come up can be a determining factor in a film's long-term success. The movie that starts strong and then loses it in Act Three, leaving the audience feeling cheated and unsatisfied, is almost a Hollywood cliché. Conversely, many movies have started slowly but gone out with a bang, resulting in positive word-of-mouth.

A good ending can also be the element that seals the deal on a screenplay. Although many a flawed script has been bought purely on the strength of its premise — the studio powers-that-be figuring they can make the story work with, oh, twenty or thirty judicious rewrites — a great last line or final image can be the kicker that causes an equivocal reader to change his recommendation from "Maybe" to "Yes," or gives the supportive D-girl the added enthusiasm she needs to call her boss at home at 10:30 PM to say, "We have to buy this script — now!"

The power of punchlines: Punchlines — pithy lines of dialogue that leave the audience laughing — are a time-tested way of going out on a strong, positive note. Such jokes can involve "running gags," a joke repeated in various forms throughout the film only to be given one last, final twist; a "call-back," a stand-up term for a joke based on a reference made earlier and likely long forgotten; or they can be humorous, ironic commentaries on the action that has just preceded them.

For example, 1987's spoof of *Dragnet*, which starred Dan Aykroyd and Tom Hanks, was a generally mediocre comedy redeemed in its final minute by a punchline that even critic Leonard Maltin described as "a howl." Throughout the film, the heroine, played by the fetching Alexandra Paul, was repeatedly referred to as "the Virgin Connie Swail." At the movie's conclusion, Aykroyd reported that he had spent the evening with "Connie Swail." "Don't you mean the Virgin Connie Swail?" Hanks inquires. Aykroyd merely cocks a knowing eyebrow, accompanied by Dragnet's famous "Dum-de-dum-dum" theme. It got the biggest laugh in the whole movie.

Particularly successful ironic comments have included Roy Scheider's line to Richard Dreyfuss at the end of 1975's *Jaws*: "Would you believe I used to be afraid of the water?" Or, in 1991's *The Silence of the Lambs*, Anthony Hopkins' Hannibal "the Cannibal" Lector telling Jodie Foster's Clarice Starling, "I'm having an old friend for dinner." Or Will Smith's line to his new bride's son as they watch the fiery remains of the alien mothership come steaming through the atmosphere like blazing meteors at the conclusion of *Independence Day* — "Didn't I say I'd show you fireworks?"

As a screenwriter, you should take advantage of an axiom stand-up comedians have known for generations: Always leave 'em laughing.

The reveal: A visual punchline can be just as effective as a verbal one. Often, this involves revealing to the audience something that has remained elusive to the characters even to the movie's end.

Arguably the most famous reveal in cinematic history is the final shot of Orson Welles' 1941 masterwork *Citizen Kane*. After everyone has spent the last 118 minutes trying to discover the meaning of the word "Rosebud," we travel through the late billionaire's massive warehouse only to discover, just as it is being consumed by flames, that "Rosebud" is the name of Kane's boyhood sled — the symbol of his lost innocence.

Other famous reveals include the partial Statue of Liberty at the end of *Planet of the Apes*, Kathleen Turner back from the dead and lounging on the beach at the end of *Body Heat*, and Kevin Spacey's eerie physical transformation from the ineffectual Verbal Kint into the criminal mastermind Keyser Soze at the conclusion of *The Usual Suspects*.

Conversely, you may wish to conclude your movie with a skillful conceal, hiding something away, as happened with the fabled Ark of the Covenant in the final shot of *Raiders of the Lost Ark*.

Lasting Impressions: Movies are well known to favor pictures over words, so a stunning final image — even one that isn't quite a "punchline" — may be just the thing you need to climax your screenplay.

For example, 1997's *The Lost World: Jurassic Park* may have been a second-rate follow-up to the original 1993 blockbuster, but its final image — that of a dozen different dinosaurs all moving gracefully through their primeval environment — was almost worth the price of admission. Likewise, the final shot of 1996's *Twister*, a dramatic pullback that revealed the incredible devastation wrought by the recent Force 5 tornado, captured in a single image the awesome power that had been perceived in bits and pieces over the previous 119 minutes.

Bookends: Sometimes, the best way to end a movie is the same way you started it. "Bookends" help bring a story full circle, whether it's the drifting feather from *Forrest Gump*, the crossroads in *Cast Away*, or life in The Shire in *The Lord of the Rings* trilogy.

The most important thing an ending can do is give a story a sense of closure. Whether it's Anthony Perkins staring weirdly into the camera at the end of *Psycho*, Steve Martin dancing with Victoria Tennant — whose mirror image reveals Lily Tomlin — in *All of Me*, or Tom Hanks and Meg Ryan standing hand-in-hand at the top of the Empire State Building in *Sleepless in Seattle*, we know at this point that the story is over and that all is once again right with the world.

Obtuse endings, where we don't know the characters' fates — a technique used in such classics as *Butch Cassidy and the Sundance Kid*, *The French Connection*, and *Thelma and Louise* — may have their place in the artist's tool chest, but they tend to leave audiences unsatisfied. Films that use this kind of ending tend to succeed in spite of, rather than because of, their lack of closure and are generally not recommended for the spec writer.

To paraphrase a famous dramatic pundit, a good ending is one that is both surprising and inevitable. Go out with a bang. Surprise us. Delight us. Wrap everything up with the kind of dramatic or comedic flourish that will distinguish you from the rest of the pack.

For that, my friend, is what screenwriting dreams are made of.

THE SALE

BACK TO THE FEATURE
Why "The End" Is Only the Beginning

So far, we've covered most aspects of spec screenplay writing. We've discussed how to choose a viable premise, structure a dramatic narrative, create vivid characters, execute a set-piece, write a slam-bang ending, and format your script to expedite the "read." By now, you've ingested all of this valuable information and, after many months of tortuous, enervating and, hopefully, occasionally orgasmic writing, you've finally finished your spec screenplay. Now you're ready to send it to producers, find a buyer, and collect your $500,000 paycheck, right?

Wrong.

The worst thing you can do to yourself and your creation is to send it into the market "hot off the printer." Why? Because writers are the worst possible judges of their own material.

After having spent weeks, months, perhaps even years honing and refining a script, you will be too close to your material to make any kind of objective analysis of its merits. There will likely be plot points that only make sense to you because you conceived them. You will no doubt love every character in your story because they are, in one way or another, reflections of yourself. The script no doubt contains jokes or zingers that you've concluded are priceless for no other reason than you spent an entire day agonizing over them. But the operative question isn't whether or not *you* think your script is great, but whether *other* people do. Especially people who are in a position to offer you a contract.

Some writers — especially new ones who are eager and impatient — opt to send their untested spec into the market and let the chips fall where they may. If they're really, really, insanely lucky, their instincts prove on-target and they find a buyer. But most writers who try this all-or-nothing approach encounter rejection and end up asking, "What didn't you like? How can I make the script better?" Which is all well and good — but once production companies have seen a script and coverage has been written, it's too late to make any changes. Unless you already have strong, established relationships, most producers will consider a script only once. If you resubmit a screenplay, even if it's been vastly rewritten, many companies will just pull their old coverage and base their decisions on that. Even changing titles and character names doesn't help you avoid this treatment. (You really can't blame studios and producers for treating writers so coldly. They're in the business of buying solid scripts, not helping desperate writers launch their careers.)

If you've spent any significant amount of time writing your screenplay, you owe it to yourself to spend just a little more time making sure it's the best script it can possibly be before tossing it to the wolves. Just as studios usually "test screen" their movies to determine what works and what doesn't, you need to "test" your script while you still have a chance to make adjustments.

Here are the steps you should take before sending your spec out to agents and/or producers:

Have your script read by at least five people whose opinions you respect. Offer your script to a mix of acquaintances — young, old, male, and female. Other writers are a great place to start. If you know people who work in the entertainment industry, even better. A professional reader or producer's assistant will be in a great position to determine how your script would be evaluated if it actually went into the market.

Although you're welcome to give you script to family members for evaluation, don't take their opinions *too* seriously, especially the positive ones. It's virtually impossible for family members to look at something written by one of their own with a cold, critical eye. And at this point in the process, you don't want praise, you want criticism.

Weigh all feedback before considering a rewrite. Although everyone is entitled to an opinion, some criticisms are more valid than others. For example, one person may find a joke you've written hilarious, while another may find the same joke flat or even offensive. One of your readers may love a character while another is unimpressed.

No, what you're looking for are not individual criticisms, but a *consensus* on what works and what doesn't. For example, if 80 percent of your readers think a certain character is flat and lifeless...chances are that the character is flat and lifeless. If one reader hates a joke but three other people love it, keep the joke. You can't please everybody. And if you absolutely, positively, from the bottom of your heart believe a certain concept, character, plot point, or piece of dialogue is 100 percent perfect and everybody else thinks it sucks, be ready to smash your delicate artistic ego like a bug and side with the majority. As a wise man once said, "If five people tell you you're drunk, it's probably time to sit down."

Hold nothing sacred. Screenwriters often become "married" to a concept, a character, or even a joke so strongly that they insist on keeping it in the script no matter what. And this is often a fatal error. Again: If you want to be a professional, the issue isn't whether or not *you* like what you've written, but if *other* people do.

Be prepared to gut entire scenes, change whole characters, or even start from page one if you have to. Nothing in a script is sacrosanct, not even the story itself. There may be times when you'll be forced to admit that, while your execution is great, your whole premise is off-base or simply uncommercial. Or you may have had a great premise but just chose to develop it in the wrong direction. Again, it's far better to get this information early, from people who'll still love you in the morning, than from hostile strangers who have no compunctions about flushing a year of your life down the toilet without so much as a fare-thee-well.

Take your time. Time is the writer's greatest enemy. We all have bills to pay. We have obligations to meet. None of us are getting any younger, and the urge to become successful *now* is, for most people, almost irresistible. It takes enormous discipline to step back, give people a chance to evaluate your material, spend the time necessary to extensively rewrite a script, and maybe even put a script away for a month or two so you can attack it with a fresh eye before finally sending it off to meet its destiny.

Discipline is exactly what it takes to make it as a professional screenwriter. The discipline to write day after day. The discipline to sit alone in a little room in front of a keyboard while those around you are actually living their lives. The discipline to keep your hopes

THE SALE

alive despite a seemingly endless stream of rejections and frustrations. So take the time it takes to make your spec the best it can possibly be.

You think rewriting your spec is tough? Hell, just wait 'til you start getting studio notes.

THE NAME GAME
What's in a Title? How About a Spec Sale?

Four hundred and fifty years ago, William Shakespeare asked, "Would a rose by any other name smell as sweet?" Perhaps, but would *Pretty Woman* have made over $100 million if it had gone by its original title, "$3,000"? Would Mel Brooks' *Blazing Saddles* have become a classic black comedy had it retained the name "Black Bart"? How much was removing the word "Alias" from the title "Alias Mrs. Doubtfire" worth to that particular production?

In Hollywood, a world where image is often more important than substance, a great title can mean tens of millions of dollars to a movie's grosses. To a writer, coming up with a memorable title can likewise mean the difference between selling a spec script or having it languish on a development executive's shelf.

Studios know the importance of titles. This is why they spend tremendous amounts of money researching the commercial viability of their products' monikers. In the case of an established franchise like *Star Trek*, *Batman*, or *Starsky & Hutch*, a well-known name virtually guarantees that mass audiences will sit up and take notice, if not in the theaters, then at least in the video stores. For an unknown property, a slam-bang title like *Showgirls* or *The Money Train* can garner strong opening weekend numbers regardless of the film's inherent quality or long-term viability.

For a non-A-list writer looking to make a sale, having a great title may not guarantee that $1 million paycheck and a three-picture deal, but it's certainly a leg up. Imagine yourself, a poor studio executive. Your job is to find that next $100 million blockbuster, and you've been given three new screenplays to read over the weekend: *Mona Lisa Smile*, *Radio*, and *Bruce Almighty*. Which script are you going to pick up first?

Granted, the rules regarding titles are just as ephemeral as every other aspect of Hollywood. Films with strong titles like *Terminal Velocity* and *Dead Men Don't Wear Plaid* can still turn out to be commercial duds, whereas ungainly titles like *Close Encounters of the Third Kind*, *Romancing the Stone*, or even *Mr. Holland's Opus* can still result in boffo box office. Still, when it comes to finding the perfect title, here are some ideas you might want to keep in mind:

Keep it short and sweet. For the most part, short titles are better than long ones. One or two words are optimum. Consider *The Matrix*, *Speed*, *Chinatown*, and *Casablanca*. When all else fails, using your main character's name can be an excellent fallback. Consider *Forrest Gump*, *Crocodile Dundee*, *The Blues Brothers*, or even *E.T.* In the case of a horror movie, you'd best be advised to use the name of the monster, á la *Dracula*, *King Kong*, *The Wolf Man*, *Gremlins*, *The Terminator*, etc.

Go for high concept. Titles that immediately encapsulate a movie's central idea are excellent attention-grabbers. Examples of this approach include, *Three Men and a Baby*, *Home Alone*, *Adventures in Babysitting*, *Back to the Future*, *Throw Momma from the Train*, *Ghostbusters*, *Jurassic Park*, and *Star Wars*. (Studio marketing departments occasionally make mistakes. Initially, Fox marketing division nixed the title *Star Wars* — figuring that, with the country still smarting from Vietnam, people didn't want to see a movie with the word "war" in the title.)

Turn a phrase. Using a common phrase relevant to your story or twisting a phrase so that it directly relates to your movie is another time-tested strategy. Some examples of this include, *Basic Instinct*, *Lethal Weapon*, *Fatal Attraction*, *Indecent Proposal*, *Presumed Innocent*, *A Few Good Men*, and *Something's Gotta Give*.

Use a song title. In the past two decades, many movies have been successfully marketed by appropriating titles of famous songs — some of which don't even appear on the movies' soundtracks. Examples of this include: *American Pie*, *Pretty Woman*, *Can't Buy Me Love*, *What's Love Got to Do With It*, *Something to Talk About*, and *Ramblin' Rose*.

Avoid long, cumbersome titles. Names like *Things to Do in Denver When You're Dead*, *Don't Be a Menace to South Central While*

Drinking Your Juice in the Hood, and *The Englishmen Who Went Up a Hill But Came Down a Mountain* may at first seem daringly original, but they tend to wear out their welcome faster than the latest Rob Schneider vehicle. Besides, you want people to be able to remember the title of your movie. When in doubt, think small.

Don't lead with your chin. You may also want to avoid titles that beg negative wisecracks, invite critical slams, or otherwise jinx your movie. For example, the remake of the 1947 noir classic *Kiss of Death* retained its original's downbeat title, and thus provided an instant headline for every critic who wanted to pan the movie. Examples of other "leading with your chin" titles: *Perfect* (it isn't), *Bill & Ted's Bogus Journey* (it was), and *Born Losers* ('nuff said).

Don't be obtuse. How many people originally avoided seeing *The Shawshank Redemption* because of its unwieldy name? Ditto *The Hudsucker Proxy*, *The Fourth Protocol*, and *Joe Versus the Volcano*. Back in 1989, MGM/UA changed the title of its new James Bond flick from *License Revoked* to *License to Kill* because they found that too many people didn't even know the meaning of the word "revoked." Again, keep it simple.

Last guys finish last. After *The Last Action Hero*, *The Last Starfighter*, *The Last Emperor*, *The Last Temptation of Christ*, *The Last Flight of Noah's Ark*, *The Last Exit to Brooklyn*, and *The Last Samurai*, let's hope we've all seen the "last" of this trend.

Remember: sex and violence sell. Take it from Joe Eszterhas, whose treatment for *One Night Stand* garnered him a cool $4 million; and David Zucker, Jim Abrahams, and Jerry Zucker who, when faced with the problem of finding a marketable name for their cop spoof, which they had based on their cult TV classic *Police Squad* back in 1988, settled on *The Naked Gun* — which they boasted "managed to fit both sex and violence into one title."

When all else fails, take it from the masters.

SCREENWRITER CALLING
Getting Your Foot in the Door

The allure of the movie business is electric. Ever since Cecil B. DeMille shot *The Squaw Man* outside a wooden barn at the intersection of modern-day Selma and Vine, would-be actors, directors, and writers have been flocking to Hollywood seeking fame and fortune. A few make it. Most don't. But they all try — and the degree of success they enjoy is often dependent on the degree of professionalism they bring to the process.

Wait a minute...! Hollywood? Professionalism? Isn't this the town where folks regularly get paid $20 million to refuse to go to work until the path between their trailer and the soundstage is strewn with rose pedals? Where business attire can consist of shorts, sandals, and a tank top (albeit a $125 tank top from Barneys)?

Yes, despite what you may have seen on *Entertainment Tonight*, the movie business *is*, first and foremost, a business. Except for a few eccentrics who manage to float their way to the top of the creative toilet bowl, the vast majority of movie industry employees are normal, educated, trained, *professional* business people. As such, they've established a business-like protocol for evaluating potential projects, one that is not all that different from the way Madison Avenue ad agencies, Chicago-area PR firms, or Kansas City-based greeting card companies find their talent. Conducting yourself in a disciplined and professional manner can be critical in getting the attention of a manager, talent agency, or production company — especially for writers, whose work must ultimately speak for itself.

So what is the "professional" way to get your screenplay in front of potential representatives and buyers? How can you make that all-important first-impression be a positive one?

Here are some tried-and-true recommendations:

Do your research. There are hundreds of talent and management agencies in the Los Angeles area, and even more producers and production entities to whom they peddle screenplays. All of them have their own operating procedures and acceptance requirements. Many specialize in particular genres. And not all of them are looking for new material or talent at any given moment.

The only way to make sure you get your material in front of people who might be receptive is to do some research. You can begin with the handful of readily available publications that list the major Hollywood talent agencies, their address and phone numbers, their acceptance requirements and, when known, the genres in which they specialize. (Perhaps the most comprehensive of these are *Fade In*'s own *Annual Agency Guide* and *Writers Guide to Hollywood Producers*. You'll also want to check out the selection of industry resource guides at an entertainment bookstore like dramabookshop.com, samuelfrench.com, or writersstore.com.)

Be sure to study each listing carefully and determine if and how you can get unsolicited material to them. Many agencies will only talk to a new writer via a referral. Likewise, many production companies — especially the larger ones — won't look at a script unless it comes to them through an accredited agent. Don't waste your time or risk your reputation by sending unsolicited scripts to companies that specifically state they won't look at scripts that arrive in this manner. It's a waste of your time and money.

Determine the submission process. Most agencies and producers will not accept "unsolicited" material. In most cases, what this really means is that they don't want hundreds of completed screenplays showing up in their mail every day. The ban against "unsolicited" material does not, however, prevent you from asking them if they will ask *you* to send them your script. In other words, all they're asking is that you make an inquiry before mailing them your screenplay.

In some directories, the agencies and production companies indicate how they want inquiries submitted (letter, phone call, email, etc.) and to whom such inquiries should be directed. They may also include prohibitions against certain media (e.g., *no emails!* — which is just as well, because email is far too easy to delete and/or ignore). If you are unsure of how to send an inquiry, send it in writing. But don't send such an inquiry by certified or registered mail. Requiring a company employee to sign a receipt for your inquiry puts an unnecessary burden on your recipient, plus is makes it look like you're giving your project far more importance than they may think it deserves.

(Quick Response Strategy: Some new writers include pre-addressed return envelopes or postcards to facilitate the response process. Although some people look upon such practices as amateurish, it has proven successful for many "undiscovered" writers. At least you may get your "No" response faster.)

Write a short, *concise* query letter. Your query letter should be targeted to an individual, not just an agency or production company. It should be no more than a page long and should contain the following information:

(1) A quick introductory greeting offering your new script (it must always be a "new" script, even if it isn't) for consideration. The opening should also demonstrate your understanding of the recipient's company and a suggestion of why your project fits his or her needs.

(2) The script's title and genre.

(3) A logline, which is a one- or two-sentence-long description of the premise. This should then be followed by a statement of the movie's theme, i.e, the provocative question or statement your story explores.

(4) Any *relevant* personal information that makes you a credible source (e.g., professional writing background, education, awards, prior sales or options, etc.)

(5) A final sentence thanking the reader for his or her time and consideration, and an expression of your eagerness to hear back in a timely manner.

Do not embellish your description with what you think the budget should be or who you think should star in it. Don't whine, complain, cajole, or threaten. Again: Be Professional.

Beware of online services. Recently, a number of online services have popped up offering to disseminate query messages via the internet or, even worse, posting your ideas online for the world to see. This is one case where high-tech is definitely high-risk.

These screenplay "registries" offer to post titles and loglines online for subscribers to peruse at their leisure in the hopes of connecting eager sellers with potential buyers. Some of these sites charge both the writer and the subscribing producers/buyers to access this service, while others allow writers to post their entries for free.

The problems with these online script registries are obvious. First, most active and credible producers don't subscribe to such services. They don't have to. They have plenty of high profile agents calling them every day pitching viable screenplays. The people who *do* subscribe are — more likely than not — wannabe producers who want to break into the business just as desperately as the writers do...and they need a script with which to do it. Second, ideas are not copyrightable, so you may very well be paying for the privilege of having someone steal your high-concept premise. Finally, online services don't leave a paper trail. If you exchange letters or emails with an agent or producer who ends up illegally appropriating all or part of your material, your written records can help support your case. You have no such recourse when your material is plucked from the ether of cyberspace.

In addition to the online registries, there are services that offer to send inquiries to potential buyers via email. Although such services may speak of targeting their inquiries, the very nature of this sort of operation indicates that they use a shotgun approach that not only rarely proves successful, but can also be damaging. (Again, most of these services just target companies, not individuals.) You don't need an online service to "blast" your ideas all over town. That's not how it's done in journalism. That's not how it's done in advertising. That's not how it's done in publishing. And that's not how it's done in the movie business.

Network! In Hollywood, no marketing is more effective than simple word-of-mouth. People who are given a script on a personal recommendation *will* read it. Fortunately, you don't need to be neighbors with Amy Pascal or Brian Grazer to plug yourself into the Hollywood pipeline. Live and work in Southern California long enough — say, thirty days — and you'll eventually meet somebody who works in some aspect of the movie business or knows someone who does. Then it's just a matter of exploiting the classic "Six Degrees of Separation" to get your script onto the desk Mr. or Ms. Right. If your script is indeed as good as you think it is, showing it

THE SALE

to enough people should eventually lead to action, be it representation, an option, or an actual sale.

And when you go to the Academy Awards, just be sure to wear your *good* tank top.

PLAYING THE GAME
What to Do When a Producer Wants to Option Your Screenplay

It's the moment every writer dreams about: You're sitting in Starbucks pounding down your third venti Columbia Narino Supremo and tapping out your "final" draft of *Spam Wrestlers from Saturn* when your cell phone rings. (Okay, it *chirps. Beeps.* Plays the entire first movement of *Beethoven's Third.* You get the idea...) It's that producer over at Sony who asked to see your last spec, *Love Don't Change a Thing.* She liked it. No, strike that; she *loved* it. She loved it so much that she wants to option it.

In a flash, everything in your world changes. The clouds part and the sun shines. The hum of traffic becomes an angelic choir. Your $4.50 cup of bean juice transforms into a glass of vintage champagne. You made it, baby. You broke through to the Big Time. You can finally pay off all those credit cards, buy that Z-car you've had your eye on, and score season tickets to the Lakers. You're gonna be rich! Rich-rich-rich!

(Insert SCREECHING BRAKES sound-effect here.)

Whoops. Reality check. The sky's still cloudy, traffic still sucks, and the closest you're gonna get to seeing Kobe from the floor is through binoculars.

An option is not a sale. It's not even the promise of a sale. But it is a necessary first step to making your Hollywood dreams come true, and it needs to be handled skillfully so you don't suffer the ol' screwgie later down the road.

First, a definition of terms. A screenplay *option* is a short-term agreement between a writer and a producer or production company in which said writer grants said producer/production company the right to "shop" (submit) said screenplay to various studios in the hopes of actually generating a purchase offer. (In today's Hollywood, big-time producers, as a rule, don't actually buy screenplays. They merely take screenplays to the larger companies that do. This is slightly different in the world of "independents" where a production company may have its own limited capital for equally limited screenplay purchases.)

Back in "the day" — say, prior to 1990 — most producers actually *paid* writers for the right to peddle their material to potential buyers. This "option price" was generally around 10 percent of the projected purchase price and kept the script "off the market" for a specified period of time, usually six months to a year. The paid option gave the producer/production company the exclusive right to seek a buyer without fear of competition.

The rationale behind the paid option was simple: On one hand, producers want exclusivity. They can't go around trying to set up a deal with a specific property when another producer is running around with the same script trying to do the same thing. On the other hand, a script that is taken all over town and rejected is essentially "burned" and unlikely to be taken seriously ever again. Since such rejection may not be based on the material per se — potential buyers may have simply not liked the producer personally and/or the talent "package" the producer had assembled — a paid option at least offers the writer some degree of compensation for his or her efforts.

About fifteen years ago, all of this changed when the pool of would-be screenwriters suddenly ballooned and producers realized that the balance of supply-and-demand was weighted heavily on their side. With so many writers screaming for attention, producers took the position that they were doing writers a favor by shopping their scripts to the studios and therefore demanded that they be given their options for free. (Hell, many writers would have *paid* producers to do it!) Under this new system, the writer gives the producer the exclusive rights to "shop" a script, and in return the producer invests the time and effort required to take it around town. Simple quid pro quo.

Today, the "free option" still rules.

Because no actual consideration is exchanged with a free option, its form and nature can vary from situation to situation. For example, if a producer is particularly tight with a specific studio — for example, if it's a producer with offices on a studio lot — then the writer can authorize the producer to shop the script to only that one studio. If the studio says no, then all rights immediately revert to the writer and he or she is free to look elsewhere.

Likewise, you can restrict an interested producer to shop the script only to a certain group of studios, and nothing beyond that. With such an arrangement, you can actually have several producers shopping the same script simultaneously, as long as their "territories" don't overlap. If two studios want the same script with different producers attached, *mazel tov*, you have a bidding war. (The one thing you want to avoid is two or more producers taking the same script to the same buyer. That's when *everybody* looks like an idiot.)

What's required to formalize a free option? Because no money is being exchanged or even promised, the agreement can be very simple. It can be a brief memo in which the terms of the option, including the time period agreed upon, are specified. Or it can be as simple as a handshake.

However, because a rejected script is still "burned" — some things *never* change — it's important that you trust the producer you're dealing with, and that the producer not violate the terms set forth in the agreement. If you agree that he'll only shop the film to Universal and Paramount but then he takes it to a half dozen other potential buyers, you're screwed. You don't want that. So be careful.

Is representation required? It couldn't hurt. If you have an agent or a manager, use him or her. It's not going to cost you anything (yet), and such professional guidance can provide invaluable down the road. (Actually, if you have an agent or manager, he or she is probably the one who found and arranged the option deal in the first place.) But since no money is yet in play, it may not pay to engage the services of an entertainment lawyer just to write up a simple free option agreement. Save the lawyer for later.

If you don't have an agent yet, this can be a great time to get one. Agents, like sharks, get excited when they smell blood, and contacting an agency with a request for help in arranging an option — even a free one — for which you've already done the legwork can be a great "in." How do you find such an agent? Ask the producer. Chances are, he or she can recommend several (and as long as it's not his or her agent, there's no reason to expect a conflict of interest).

Should you and your producer discuss a purchase price at this time? Sometimes ballpark figures are discussed, as well as general terms (right to first rewrite, etc.), but all of this goes out the window when a studio actually steps up to the plate and the war between the agents and Business Affairs begins. The best advice is to play it cool. Don't even mention money yet. You could look too greedy — or your figure could actually be too *low* — so you might as well just leave that issue for the appropriate time and place.

The most important thing to remember when someone wants to option your material is to *stay cool*. Don't rush out and buy a new car or start treating all your friends to filet mignon at Morton's. Don't tell your family that you just sold a screenplay (you haven't yet) or even allow yourself to entertain all but the most modest of hopes that you actually will. The sad fact is that most options don't amount to anything. Scripts get "shopped" and dropped like sitcoms on the WB. Even with an A-List producer on your side, the odds are still against you.

But an option is still an essential step toward making a sale, and there's a huge ego boost that comes from having a bona fide producer validate your work. The trick is to recognize an option for what it is and treat it accordingly. Make sure you're dealing with someone trustworthy. Make sure the terms of the option are understood by all parties involved. Get money if you can (good luck). And then sit back and watch the dice roll.

An option — even a free option — means you're officially in the game. And who knows, this time around you just might hit the jackpot.

CODE OF CONDUCT
What Hollywood Expects From You Before, During, and After You Sell Your Screenplay

People are attracted to the film business for any number of reasons. Some see the cinema as a vehicle for artistic expression. Some are motivated by dreams of celebrity. And others come looking for nothing more than unimaginable wealth.

Regardless of why people come to Hollywood, one perception shared by virtually all rookies is that this is a laid back town where glitz and glamour rule, where eccentricity is not only tolerated but encouraged, and that the person with the biggest ego wins. This "anything goes" mystique is promulgated, in large part, by the tabloid press, its electronic counterparts (*Entertainment Tonight*, *Extra*, the *E!* network), and by the wildly skewed movies that Hollywood creates about itself (*Bowfinger*, *The Player*, *Swimming with Sharks*, *The Big Picture*, *Irreconcilable Differences*, etc).

Like all stereotypes, the popular image of Hollywood as a gilded insane asylum populated by wild-eyed, designer clad, Porsche driving, coke sniffing, silicone enhanced, idol worshipping egomaniacs contains a kernel of truth. There are plenty of obscenely rich whack-jobs roaming the studios environs of Burbank, Century City, Culver City, and Hollywood proper. But, should the stars align and the Celluloid Gods smile upon you, you should not — repeat *not* — use any of these club hopping, intern abusing, DUI collecting, vein popping media-hogs as your behavioral role models. In fact, if you want to be taken seriously by Hollywood's power brokers and launch a career that's going to be around longer than an *American Idol* winner's debut CD, you *must* conduct yourself in a manner that satisfies your employer's needs and promotes trust in your professional and personal competence.

Here, then, are some guidelines for your professional conduct before, during, and after selling your first screenplay:

Before: Your spec screenplay is completed. You've found an agent/manager/entertainment lawyer who has agreed to represent it. Obviously, you want to get your opus into the hands of every top producer, director, and star in town *now* and spark a bidding war that will net you that cool million you've always dreamed about. So you give your agent/manager/entertainment lawyer a "short list" of fifty or so A-list players, then park yourself in front of that wide-screen plasma TV (that you plan to pay for with your new-found fortune), with your cell phone clutched in your sweaty palm in preparation for the every-fifteen-minute updates you intend to demand from your representative.

Okay, boys and girls, what's wrong with this picture?

To begin, before your script can even go into the marketplace, your representative is going to need copies. If you're represented by a major agency like William Morris, ICM, CAA, Endeavor, UTA, etc., they will most likely produce the copies themselves. They have the equipment, the labor, and the budget to do it all on-site. However, if you're represented by a medium-sized or "boutique" agency, your agent may ask you provide the copies yourself. Don't protest. Make the stupid copies. There are plenty of copy shops in Hollywood and The Valley that offer very reasonable rates for this sort of thing — they cater to budget-strapped neophytes like yourself — and you can probably produce all the copies your representative will need for $100 to $150. Just keep the receipt for your taxes. You may need the write-off.

Next, although you may dream of getting your screenplay directly into the hands of Steven Spielberg, James Cameron, Michael Bay, or Peter Jackson, trust your representatives' expertise in this area. Chances are they have particular relationships with specific actors, directors, producers, and production companies — buyers who already trust their judgment — so allow your reps to first take this path of least resistance, especially if you're looking to secure your first screen sale. You can work *with* your representative to develop a distribution list, but don't presume to know more than your rep does. If you did, you wouldn't need a rep. (And you do need a rep.)

Once the script goes out, it's okay to call your representative every other day at the end of business to get a status report. However, if you make such calls, prepare yourself for bad news. If there was any *good* news to report, your representative would have called. *Immediately.* See, agents, managers, and entertainment lawyers are people, too. Honest. And they hate rejection just as much as you do. The difference is, because they're handling maybe thirty clients at a time, they have to put up with *thirty times* the rejection you do as an individual. When *good* news comes along, they're just as eager to share it with you as you are to receive it. Giving you good news makes *them* feel better — it validates their work — so they're not going to hesitate to report even the most modest of positive reactions.

So the best thing to do when a script goes out is to forget about it. Watch TV. Go to a movie. Volunteer at a local homeless shelter. Even work on your next script. Don't go out and buy toys with money you don't yet have and don't bug your representative every fifteen, thirty, or sixty minutes for updates. The old expression "Don't call us, we'll call you" was created for just this situation, so pay it heed and think about something else, however difficult that may be.

Just keep your cell phone charged. You never know when lightning's gonna strike.

During: This is when things get interesting. Someone has stepped up to the plate and expressed interest in making your movie. An offer is made, you negotiate, then you sign the papers, and deposit your big fat paycheck. What could be easier?

Perhaps a root canal.

In most cases, here's what *really* happens, and what others will expect from you during the process.

First, a producer/production company will express interest in *optioning* your script. Not buying, *optioning.* That means that they want you to grant them some degree of exclusivity for a set amount of time so they can "shop" your script to actual buyers without fear that someone else is doing the exact same thing.

In years past, options usually involved paying the writer cold hard cash for "taking the script off the market" during the option period. No more. In most cases, producers will want a *free* option, your only compensation being the knowledge that a bona fide producer/production company is actually putting his/her/their reputation on the line by attaching themselves to your project.

If a free option is requested, grant it. You may ask your agent to *try to* get some remuneration, but don't make a federal case of it. There will be plenty of other bigger hills ahead for you to die on, should you be so inclined.

Next, the producer/production company may want to meet with you to discuss your script before formalizing your agreement. Take the meeting. Show up on time. Dress nicely. (Don't overdress — but don't arrive in sweaty gym clothes, either.) *Listen* to what the producer/production company has to say (they may see substantial rewrites down the road) and always be pleasant and polite. Essentially, this is a job interview, so act accordingly.

Whatever you do, *don't* discuss money. Don't bring up the subject, and if the producer does, just say, "My agent/manager/lawyer handles all that." This will make everyone immediately feel more comfortable. Even you.

At this point, the producer may ask you to perform a "polish rewrite" on your script before submitting it, incorporating changes he or she would like to see. Whether or not to do a "free rewrite" is really up to you. If you like the ideas you've been given, you may want to incorporate them just to improve your script. (you still own all the rights at this point). If you don't like the suggestions — if you don't agree with the direction this producer wants to take your project — you may choose to pass on the idea altogether. Or you may simply say, "It sounds interesting. I'll definitely think about it," and then have your representative later inform the producer that you'll be happy to perform any rewrites after formal contracts have been executed.

Essentially, your role at this time is always to be the helpful, positive collaborator. Leave any "dirty work" to your representative. That's how he or she earns that 10 percent of your paycheck.

Once you and your producer/production company have decided to do business together, an option agreement will likely be drawn up. If you're not working with a lawyer yet, you may want to get one at this point. Make sure all of the producer's responsibilities and limitations are spelled out in the agreement. An ounce of prevention early on can be worth tens of thousands of dollars in lawsuits should things go south later.

Now you're back to playing the waiting game as your new producer begins shopping your script to studios. Again, just try to put it out of your mind. It's out of your hands now — incessant phone calls or badgering aren't going to make anyone work any harder or faster. If the phone rings, answer. Otherwise, focus your mind elsewhere.

If your phone *does* ring and you have a studio offer, things will get *very* interesting *very* quickly. First, you and your producer will probably be asked to attend a meeting with the production executives who have been assigned to your movie. As before, dress nicely, show up on time, listen to suggestions, nod and smile a lot, and never, ever discuss terms. (If you discuss money at this point, your agent will *kill* you. I'm serious about this. You will be *murdered in your sleep*.) If all goes right and the studio doesn't perceive you as a total ass, then you will hear the loveliest words in the English language: "Your agent will get a call from Business Affairs tomorrow."

And now for another warning: Contract negotiations can take forever. This is especially true if your contract and your producer's contract are being hammered out simultaneously by different sets of attorneys. It's quite possible that you will be asked to start rewrites before you actually have a contract in place. If your agent feels that you're on safe ground, do it. Don't hold up the creative process on legal technicalities. The money will come. Eventually. Again, don't spend the money before the check clears.

At some point, a contract will be finalized. Make sure your lawyer reviews it carefully and that no questions remain unanswered. Sign the document, then go get drunk. You've earned it.

After: This is the part of the process we all look forward to, and it's where many young writers get into serious trouble. Being a *paid* screenwriter, especially at the studio level, can be a powerful psychological intoxicant. A sense of *entitlement* imbues many the first-time screenwriter with a degree of ego-inflation that can, if left unchecked, make he or she insufferable.

The trick here is to focus on the work. Show up on time to scheduled meetings. Try to deliver material at the required times. Always remain available to take calls and stay receptive to suggestions. Don't disappear for days on end and not tell anyone where you are. (Yes, this happens.) (*Often.*)

However, keep in mind that while you are now being paid, that does not obligate you to take every suggestion you're given. If you don't like a proposed change, try to understand the perceived problem the studio is trying to fix and, if their concerns are legitimate, develop a better, alternative solution. If you believe the concern isn't legitimate, make a case for that, too. (At the studio level, many suggestions are made for their own sake and their originators will quickly back down if a logical counter-argument is advanced.)

As a first-time writer, be prepared to be re-written by someone else. If you turn in a script and don't hear back from the studio within a few weeks, it probably means they've decided to hire someone to replace you. Let it go. You got your check. Enjoy your money. Write something else. Don't let your ego send you into a fit of self-defeating rage. If your work was truly as good as you think it was, the studio may ultimately call you back if your replacement fails to deliver, and you don't want to have burned any bridges in the interim.

When all is said and done, just remember that the operative word in show business is *business*, and it's important to conduct yourself as you would in any other professional field. Be courteous. Be responsible. Be honest.

Such behavior may not make headlines, but, hey, screenwriters are never profiled on *Extra* anyway.

PITCH ME A WINNER
The Tricks of the Trade

Mention "pitching" to a group of working screenwriters and you'll get a reaction akin to bringing up Iraq during a French wine tasting party. It's controversial. To many screenwriters, reducing a complex screen story to a fifteen-minute oral presentation is akin to jogging through the Metropolitan Museum of Art; you may hit all the high points, but you'll miss all the nuance. To the more mercenary among us, pitching is a way to secure mega-buck deals without having to actually do any work. (The nasty downside being that one's follow-through must then meet — or exceed — the expectations you've established.) But for those who really know their craft, pitching can be an effective way to make sure a story actually works before investing months — or even years — trying to bring it to life.

Whatever your personal view of pitching, the fact remains that it's a key skill that every screenwriter needs to develop. The most in-demand A-List writers may spend half their days pitching projects — both original and solicited. Writers who have just sold their first specs will need to pitch follow-up projects just to maintain their initial momentum. And novices making their first rounds of Hollywood producers and development execs will encounter the inevitable questions, "What else have you got?" — and God help the newbie who doesn't have a well-rehearsed response.

Pitching is not quite as intimidating as it may initially sound. True, a natural actor or orator may "give better pitch" than a soft-spoken introvert. But with the proper preparation, guidance, and practice, even the most neurotic, tongue-tied scribe can give a professional-level pitch that achieves the exercise's primary objective: to make a potential buyer excited about your screenplay.

What kind of projects get pitched? Everything. People pitch magazine articles, unfinished novels, old TV shows, one-man stage-plays, stand-up comedy routines, and, yes, even finished screenplays. The purpose of the pitch may be to get a production company to turn an idea into a screenplay, or it may be to get a studio to turn a screenplay into a movie. But whatever the source material or the immediate goal, pitching always boils down to the same thing: Telling a story.

Here, then, are the basic elements that every effective pitch should contain — and the order in which they should be presented:

Title: Yes, your project needs a title. A great title can get listeners excited immediately. Again, a title should be short and it should be catchy. If possible, it should capture the story's premise or theme. It may be a common expression or even a song title. (And no, you don't need the rights to use a song as a screenplay title.) And it shouldn't sound like any other well-known title. Examples of great titles include, *Jaws*, *Home Alone*, *Indecent Proposal*, *Fatal Attraction*, *Panic Room*, and *Phone Booth*. Recently, the market has been glutted by films with some very weak titles, including *Tears of the Sun* (sounds like a chick flick), *Basic* (sounds simple), *What a Girl Wants* (not to be confused with *What Women Want*), and *The Life of David Gale* (I don't know who David Gale is, why should I care about his life?). Come up with a great title and you're already halfway home.

Genre: What kind of a movie is this? A romantic comedy? An urban action picture? A historical drama? You need to identify the drama to establish expectations. If your story is a comedy, the listeners know it's okay to laugh. If it's a tearjerker, then the listeners will expect to cry. You may wish to further classify your film by comparing it to similar movies the listeners may be aware of. If you're going to do this, here are the guidelines: (1) Use at least *three* examples of similar films ("It's a romantic comedy in the vein of *Maid in Manhattan*, *Two Weeks Notice*, and *Sweet Home Alabama*.); (2) The examples you use should all have been hits, and (3) Don't reference films that are more than five or six years old. Saying, "It's an adventure film like *Gunga Din*, *The African Queen*, and *King Solomon's Mines*" will get you nothing but blank stares.

Premise: A good movie premise should be able to be clearly expressed in one or two sentences. While some have derided the whole idea of the "high concept" as being cheap and artless, the fact is that simple stories tend to appeal to both producers and to audiences — and they're much easier to write! However, keep in mind that "simple" doesn't mean "simplistic." A good premise needs to be fresh and original with plenty of inherent conflict and, if possible, a clever "twist" on convention. A little irony doesn't hurt either.

Example #1 — *Gladiator.* "Rome's greatest general is falsely accused of treason, his wife and son are murdered, and he's sold into slavery. Thrust into gladiatorial combat, he quickly becomes a national hero and is able to challenge the very emperor who betrayed him."

Example #2 — *A Beautiful Mind.* "In the midst of the Cold War, a socially awkward genius on the verge of a mathematical breakthrough struggles to separate fantasy from reality when he's besieged by bouts of schizophrenia."

Example #3 — *Chicago.* "In 1920s Chicago, a would-be chorus girl uses the press to turn a charge of murder into a ticket to celebrity. And it's a musical."

All simple premises. And all Best Picture winners.

Theme: Theme addresses the question, "What is this movie *about?*" What is the larger question being asked? What is the lesson the hero learns? In short, what's the *point?* Themes can be simple ("love conquers all," "good vs. evil," "be yourself") or they can be complex ("he who saves one life saves the world," "love *doesn't* always conquer all"). Whatever your theme is, you have to know it and be able to express it *quickly.* One sentence. Then it's time to move on to...

Your story: This is the heart of the pitch. Like the movie you intend to write (or have already written), your story is going to have a beginning, a middle, and an end. It is, in fact, going to be your movie told in the way you intend for the story to unfold on the screen. And as such, you want to be as specific as possible. You want to tell your story in terms of *images* and *actions.* When you begin your story, describe the first shot. What's happening? Who is the hero, and what does he do that makes us care about him or her? Continue to tell your story in terms of *specific* actions, locations, problems, solutions, and, perhaps most important of all, *emotions.* Tell your story in a way that brings out the *feelings* your story is intended to generate.

Set-pieces: Perhaps even more important than the story itself are the set-pieces you've created to flesh it out. If you've started with a simple premise, your plotline is also probably pretty simple; it's the set-pieces that will bring it to life. For example, if you were going to pitch the unexpected comedy mega-hit *My Big Fat Greek Wedding*, you wouldn't concentrate on the familiar "girl-meets-boy" storyline. No, you'd pitch set-pieces: Gus explaining how every English word comes from Greek; Ian flirting with Toula through the window of the travel agency; Ian's uptight WASP parents coming to have dinner with the Portokoloses, only to find fifty drunk Greeks roasting a lamb on the front lawn; the elder Millers learning to drink ouzo, etc. Those are the scenes that sold the movie to audiences; these are the same scenes you'd promote to sell the film to prospective producers.

The big finish: Build to your climax, then wrap things up fast. Again, don't just tell the listener how things turn out — *show* them with images and actions. It's been said that people remember the first lines of novels and the last scenes of movies. What's your last scene? Is it memorable? If not, *make* it memorable. How your listener feels when your pitch is over will often determine if you have a sale or not.

That is the structure of a perfect pitch. It's your movie, expressed in a series of scenes strung together in linear fashion with clear cause-and-effect relationships. It's a verbal "coming attractions" clip that, if done right, captures the emotional and thematic essence of the movie you imagine.

Here are a few other general guidelines on "giving good pitch":

Keep it short. A good pitch should be no more than fifteen to twenty minutes.

Rehearse, rehearse, rehearse. When you're giving a pitch, you're essentially performing a one-man show. This being the case, you need to be as smooth, confident, and prepared as any stand-up comic. You have to know your material backwards and forwards and be able to jump into the story at any point, because...

Be prepared to be interrupted. Unlike a one-man show, a pitch is not a one-way presentation. A prime objective of this exercise is to engage your listeners, to prompt them to respond, ask questions, even give suggestions. The more the "pitchee" gets involved in your story, the more that story becomes *his* (or hers), and such an investment often leads directly to a sale.

Don't argue. If the listener objects to any part of your story — including your premise — don't argue. Never become defensive or, worse yet, combative. If the listener brings up a hole in your story, just say, "You're right. We gotta fix that..." and then get right back to the action. If, when you're done, a producer says, "That's great, but we've got something just like it in development," don't insist that your story is *different*. Just say, "I understand. May I come back later with something else?" If you've done your job well, the answer will be "Yes."

Don't leave anything behind. Often, you will be asked to leave a synopsis behind. Don't. You're there to pitch, not submit synopses. Let the development exec pass the story along himself; with luck, he'll do it in a way he knows will excite his superior. In effect, by not submitting a synopsis, you force the exec to go to work for you. And that's a good position to be in.

Don't overstay your welcome. Get in, get out, and always leave 'em wanting more.

Kind of like this chapter.

AGENT, SCHMAGENT
The Do-It-Yourself Script Sale

"You gotta have an agent."

In Hollywood, it's as familiar a mantra as, "We're big fans of yours." At screenwriting seminars, where industry professionals come to share their accumulated wisdom, the first question a neophyte scribe inevitably poses is never, "How do I round out a character?" or "How do I avoid story predictability?" but always, "How do I get an agent?"

And among those writers who *have* agents, the plaintive cry is usually, "How do I get a *better* agent?"

All right, then, here's the God's honest truth about agents. They can be very useful in negotiating deals. And they're invaluable when it comes to getting a shot at studio writing assignments. But here's the dirty little secret no agent will admit: If you have a great spec script, you don't need an agent to find a buyer. Yes, you may need a savvy representative to pound out a deal once a buyer expresses interest, but you can make that all-important first sale, the one that sets you on that Yellow Brick Road to screenwriting stardom, all by yourself.

The Do-It-Yourself Script Sale is actually a pretty simple process. Simple, but not easy. (Nothing worthwhile is ever easy.) Here are the steps you need to take:

Write a great script. This is by far the most difficult part of the whole process. Yes, every writer *thinks* they write great scripts, but if that were actually the case, we'd have never been subjected to *Slackers* and *Rollerball*. (And those are scripts that got made. Imagine the scripts that didn't.) How do you know if you've written a great script? Easy. *People tell you.* And not your mother and not your significant other. *Real* people. People in the industry. People who read scripts for a living and have solid criteria against which to judge your work. This, of course, requires you to know such people — which isn't all that difficult if you've spent any time at all in the Los Angeles area, where it seems that *everybody* is in show business. In other words, if you live in SoCal, join writers groups, attend screenwriting seminars, and do whatever else it takes to make contacts and develop a network of trusted industry-savvy advisors and sounding boards. And if you don't live in Southern California, contact someone who *does* and see if he or she can get your script read by people who know what the hell they're talking about.

Finally, take advantage of a reputable, professional coverage service. Staffed by industry professionals who are experienced in the vagaries of the modern motion picture business, such a service can provide you with critical insights into how to make your screenplay more artistically and commercially viable — *before* sending it out to potential buyers.

Identify your market. In the above paragraph, you were advised to write a great script. However, what constitutes "great" is highly dependent on what kind of product a particular producer is looking for. And, make no mistake; movies are a "product" — a commodity manufactured to satisfy the demands of a vast worldwide consumer market — in this case the demand for entertainment. Different producers look for different kinds of projects and judge them accordingly. Just as there are "great" burgers as well as "great" bottles of wine, your lowbrow teen sex comedy may be "great" by its genre's standards in the same way a Jane Austen adaptation may be "great" by its own. Your challenge is to properly classify your screenplay, judge it against other projects of its type, and then pursue those buyers who are most likely to respond positively to its content.

Locate potential buyers. Your next step is to do exactly what an agent would do: Identify producers who are in a position to buy your script. In the best of all possible worlds there would be a printed list of just such candidates, complete with addresses and phone numbers, whom you could contact directly. Handily, dramabookshop.com, samuelfrench.com, and writersstore.com are three superlative websites that carry a host of industry resource guides. Make sure that the one you purchase gives you studio and production company names, contact names, phone numbers and addresses, and the genres they're looking for. This last piece of data is critical because it gives you a good idea of the kind of movies each company prefers to produce. Obviously, if you have a grim period piece, you're not going to approach a producer whose last project was *Mud Wrestlers from Venus*.

Prepare your pitch. All magic tricks require intense preparation, and selling a screenplay is no exception. Your goal is to boil your story down to one or two powerful sentences that will really excite the listener. This is why so-called "high concept" stories make such good first-time screenplays; they're designed to be sold in a single "logline." Such an approach may seem simplistic to those writers who prefer their stories deep and complex, but remember: Producers are busy people and often have short attention spans. They're not interested in sitting through a long spiel. They want "the poster." So give it to them. Be able to say, "This is a movie about...," and make it exciting before you have to take another breath. It's not as difficult as it sounds, even for "serious" films. For example, here's how you might pitch some Academy Award-worthy screenplays:

A Beautiful Mind: "It's a love story about a world-class mathematical genius and his beautiful student — and the guy turns out to be a paranoid schizophrenic. Oh, and it's a true story."

The Royal Tennenbaums: "It's a comedy about what happens to a dysfunctional family of kid geniuses when they all grow up."

Gosford Park: "It's an Agatha Christie-style murder mystery meets *Upstairs, Downstairs*."

You need to be able to pitch your project just as succinctly.

Get your foot in the door. Now you start cold-calling. Do you immediately call Paramount Pictures? Of course not. Studios are the *last* step in the sales process. They only buy scripts that are brought to them by producers they want to do business with. So your job is to go for the producers. They may be "on the lot" or in Van Nuys, or wherever. It doesn't matter. Once you have your resource guide in your hand, start making your inquiries. You can do this by mail, by email, or by telephone. Use whatever method with which you're most comfortable. (Many writers prefer the written word over vocal contact because, well, they're *writers*.) Whichever method you choose, the general approach is still the same. Give the company your name, explain that you are a screenwriter, and that you would very much like a chance to submit a (insert genre here) screenplay you've just completed for their consideration. Give them your log-line. Then, if this is a written communication, thank them for their time and say you look forward to hearing from them soon, etc.

Here are some critical points to remember when making your pitch:

Only pitch one script to a particular company at any one time. If the company says they're looking for romantic comedies, action films, and science fiction movies, then send them a romantic come-dy *or* an action film *or* a science fiction movie. But never send all three. You'll just muddy the waters and confuse them.

Don't demand that the producer read your script him- or her-self. Selling a screenplay is always about finding a champion. Producers champion scripts to studios, and readers/story analysts/story editors champion screenplays to producers. So start at the bottom. You'll actually have a better chance of getting to the top that way.

Sign the release form. Many producers require unrepresented writers to sign a release promising not to sue them if they eventual-ly produce movies that contain material similar to yours. Do it. No matter what you sign, you're not granting anyone permission to steal from you, so don't worry about plagiarism issues. If they *do* really and truly steal your stuff (and this rarely happens), you will still have every right to pursue legal redress.

What if the company says they only take scripts from accredited agents? Then things get more difficult. Not impossible, but more difficult. The key to winning in this situation is to remember that Hollywood is a town built on relationships. Friends trump policies in every situation. So make a friend. Like the development execu-tive's assistant. Call him or her up personally and say, "Hi. I know your company policy is not to take scripts from unrepresented writ-ers, but I was wondering — may I send *you* my script to read, and then maybe you can tell me what you think of it?" Very likely the lowly assistant wants to be producer him- or herself someday and will be flattered and agree. And if he or she likes your work, ta-da, now you have a champion.

Leave it to the Gods. Once you've made your best effort and one or more producers have your script in hand, let Fate take its course. Don't harass your potential buyers with follow-up calls or emails asking for "updates" on how your script is being received. If they like it, they'll let you know. If they don't, there's not a damned thing you can do to change their minds. If you must have some clue as to how they reacted, include a self-addressed stamped envelope when you send in your script. In most cases, your script will be returned, which is a pretty good clue that they decided to pass. Sometimes they'll even include a note explaining why...in the most polite of terms, of course.

And if they like your script? And they take it to a studio that wants to buy it? *That's* when you can go to CAA, William Morris, Endeavor, or UTA, and say, "Universal wants to buy my screenplay, and I need someone to negotiate for me."

And that, dear student, is how you get an agent.

THE SECRETS

ISN'T IT IRONIC?
Irony Isn't Dead — It Just Went to the Movies

The premise is the cornerstone of all screenwriting. Begin with a great premise and the screenplay practically writes itself. Have a weak premise and all the knowledge of structure, character development, dialogue, and formatting in the world won't save you. So important is premise that many a screenplay pitch has sold on this element alone. Is a good premise worth its weight in gold? No — it's worth more. *Much* more.

Like all great things, great movie premises are few and far between. That's one reason they're so valuable. However, while great ideas may be elusive, a premise that is at least good is actually easier to come up with than you might think. And sometimes, with the right execution, "good" can become "great."

So what is the benchmark of a good movie premise? A good premise contains immediately recognizable elements of conflict, surprise, obstruction, and the potential for character growth. In other words, all those things we go to the movies to enjoy.

Although these elements appear somewhat far-reaching, they can, in fact, be reduced to a single word: irony.

Since September 11th, we've been told that irony is dead. Far from it. Irony is not only alive and well, it's been that way since the dawn of human history. Virtually all great stories, from Homer's *Iliad* to Shakespeare's *Romeo and Juliet* and Orson Welles' *Citizen Kane*, have reveled in it. Irony is the heart and soul of drama. Without it, drama — like comedy — doesn't work.

Exactly what is dramatic irony? Mr. Webster defines irony as "incongruity between the actual result of a sequence of events and the normal or expected result." In other words, *surprise*. If you have a situation where one outcome is expected and the exact opposite occurs (sometimes called "the old switcheroo"), congratulations: you've got irony.

When it comes to dramatic characters, irony tends to occur when their circumstances or behavior are in direct conflict with their professions or stations in life.

For example:
• The doctor who becomes sick...
• The dancer who becomes paralyzed...
• The fashion model who becomes disfigured...
• The millionaire who goes bankrupt...
• The homeless person who wins the lottery...
• The nobody who saves the world...

These are all classic ironies, and they just reek of dramatic/comic potential.

Look at some recent top-grossing movies and Oscar winners. Virtually all of them had ironic premises:

A Beautiful Mind — The story of a schizophrenic genius. His mind was both his greatest asset and his greatest enemy. *Irony!*

The Lord of the Rings — The fate of the world rests in the hands of the smallest and meekest of creatures. *Irony!*

Training Day — A top narcotics cop turns out to be the biggest crook of all. *Irony!*

Monster's Ball — A woman falls in love with a man, not realizing he's responsible for executing her late husband. *Irony!* Plus, she's black...and he's a racist! *Double irony!*

In movies, irony often comes from the clash of extremes: The slob and the fussbudget (*The Odd Couple*), the family man and the psycho (*Lethal Weapon*), city and country (*Crocodile Dundee*), master and servant (*Gosford Park*).

What's the highest-grossing picture of all time? *Titanic*. It's not just a story about an "unsinkable" ship that sinks (irony #1), it's the story of the world's *largest* ship (irony #2) that sinks *on its maiden voyage* (irony #3) as told through the eyes of two lovers who come from opposite ends of the social spectrum (irony #4).

With so many ironic elements, it's no wonder the picture grossed more than a billion dollars worldwide.

How can you develop your own ironic premise? Here are some simple guidelines:

Try to work in extremes. Develop a leading character who represents the ultimate version of some characteristic. He's the world's worst (fill in the blank). She's the world's best (fill in the blank). He has the most (fill in the blank). She has the least (fill in the blank). Of course, your characters may not "technically" be the world's best/worst/biggest/smallest/first/last anything, but this exercise is bound to point you in the right direction.

Put extreme characters in direct conflict. The best with the worst. The fearful with the fearless. The prince with the pauper. The militant feminist with the male chauvinist pig. Not only do such conflicts present immediate dramatic possibilities (i.e., conflict), they also give each character the pressure he or she needs to grow.

Look for "The Least Likely To..." When a cop solves a murder, that's not drama; that's a procedural. When the victim comes back from the dead to solve his *own* murder...now that's interesting. Always look for unlikely heroes, for long-shot champions, for ordinary people thrust into extraordinary situations.

Make sure you can express your ironic premise simply and eloquently. "The Slobs Against the Snobs" (*Caddyshack*). "Sam Stone's wife has just been kidnapped...and he doesn't want her back!" (*Ruthless People*). "The general who became a slave; the slave who became a gladiator; the gladiator who defied an emperor" (*Gladiator*).

Call it the "twist," the "gimmick," or even the "high concept," it is the element of irony that propels most, if not all, successful stories.

Some writers take their entire lifetimes searching for this simple truth, yet it's been staring us in the face for more than 5,000 years.

Now isn't that ironic?

AS GOOD AS IT GETS?
When "Good Enough" Isn't

Back in 1973, New York theater critic John Lahr published a book titled, *Astonish Me: Adventures in Contemporary Theatre.* The book's central premise was that, having "seen it all," modern audiences were no longer content with merely "competent" stageplays. Plays needed to shock. To excite. To surprise. In short, jaded theater-goers no longer wished to be merely entertained. They wanted to be *astonished!*

Although more than thirty years have passed since Lahr wrote his treatise, his maxim is more relevant than ever. Especially to first-time screenwriters. In this highly competitive industry, technical competency by itself will not secure you an agent, nor will it lead to a spec sale or writing assignment. You can structure backwards and forwards, have all your "plot points" and "reversals" on precisely the right pages, write fully-dimensional characters, sparkling dialogue, creative action set-pieces, and even format your script with mathematical perfection, but unless you can *astonish* your readers, chances are your efforts will yield little more than a bad case of carpal tunnel syndrome.

This demand for "genius" is a standard many unproduced writers find extremely frustrating to face. After all, with all the dreck oozing its way out of the major studios and TV networks these days (can anyone say *From Justin to Kelly?*), one would think that competency alone would get one noticed. For if, in the Land of the Blind, the one-eyed-man is king — then in the Land of the Bland, surely the good writer should be emperor (at the very least).

Alas, such is not the case. The cold truth is, agents and producers aren't looking for good writers. They already *have* "good" writers. In fact, they have more "good" writers than they know what to do with. But while you may be just as "good" as any of these "good" writers, they'll always have one thing you don't: *A track record.* And in a business motivated by fear, uncertainty, and the ever-present need to pass the buck in the event of failure, credits — good *or* bad — will always trump talent.

So if "good enough" isn't, what is a writer to do? How can you, as a writer, determine if your writing is "great"? And if it isn't, what can you do to make it so?

Although there's no substitute for "genius" — or any way to teach it, for that matter — here are some steps you can take to try to help your screenplay blow the socks off its readers:

Test market your premise. In Hollywood, no commodity is more valuable than a good idea. More than fifteen years after the phrase "High Concept" was coined, the demand for a premise that "writes itself" is still as hot as ever — especially in the spec market. To determine whether or not you have a "hot" idea, boil your idea down to one or two sentences (a logline) and test it out on your really, really good friends. (Defined as people you can trust not to steal your really, really good idea.) Tell them, "I'm writing a movie about *such-and-such,*" and watch their reactions. If they nod, smile politely, and say, "Gee, sounds great. Good luck," then you know you might as well move on to something else. But if their eyes get that far-away look and you can almost hear the wheels turning in their heads, or if they slap their palms to their foreheads in a "Man, why didn't *I* think of that!" gesture, then you know you're onto something big. Start writing immediately.

Look for similarities between your idea and other successful films. For more than a decade now, a popular way to come up with new movie ideas has been to create a "meet." As in, "It's *Titanic* meets *Spider-man,*" or "It's *Die Hard* meets *Bridget Jones's Diary.*" The variation on this is the "only." As in, "It's *Gladiator,* only in space," or "It's *The Dirty Dozen,* only with girls." If you can play this game with *your* premise, junk it. In the vast majority of cases, the best such a "formula" premise will produce is a "formula" screenplay, and we're trying to do better than that, right? Obviously, your script will probably fall into some established genre category (*Pulp Fiction* was a "gangster film," and *Memento* is a "film noir"), but you want it to be as fresh and unusual as you possibly can. You want your film to be the one other scripts *are compared to*, not vice-versa.

Don't trust your instincts. This may seem counter-intuitive to good writing, but the truth is that what most people call "instincts" are actually "reflexes." We've all been exposed to so many thousands of hours of television and motion picture stories over our lifetimes that, when confronted with a dramatic situation, our first reaction is to solve the problem the same way we've seen it solved dozens of times before. (Even if the classic solution never really made sense to begin with.) When trying to *astonish* your audience, take your first instinct, examine it for flaws or clichés, then throw it out and force yourself to come up with a solution or approach you've never seen before. If it takes you two weeks — great. For if it took *you* two weeks to solve the problem, then chances are your audience won't figure it out in the few moments they have to ponder it.

Research. Many writers hate to research. They're writers. They want to *write*. And while they may write well, all anyone can write about is what they're familiar with. Which, in too many cases, are other movies. A great way to avoid this trap is to research your subject matter. Deeply. Chances are, you'll unearth ideas, situations, characters, problems, and solutions you would never have thought of if left only to our own imagination. Research is also a wonderful defense. You can justify even the most bizarre plot twist with "Based on a true story."

Go for broke. A problem common to even experienced writers is timidity. They're afraid to think big. "This'll be too expensive," they think. Or, "It's too far out." Don't let practical concerns get in the way of telling a good story. These days, anything can be put on the screen. If what you've written *is* too expensive or too grotesque, or too sexy, that will be worked out in rewrites. So swing for the fences. Push that envelope. Don't write funny. Write *hilarious*. Don't write scary. Write *terrifying*. Don't write big. Write *huge*. Don't write erotic. Write *orgasmic.* Take no prisoners.

Take your act on the road. When your script is finished, do your damnedest to stage a live reading of your material before a substantial audience (ten or more people) before giving it to an agent or producer. If you've written a comedy, listen for the laughs. If you've written a horror film, listen for the groans and watch people squirm. If you've written a tear-jerker, listen for the sniffles. Has your story grabbed the audience? Are they paying attention? Are they captivated? Are they *into your movie?* Professional comics always test new material and cut it mercilessly when necessary. You need to be just as ruthless.

Obviously, writing "great" instead of just "good" is a daunting task. Which is why so many "good" writers never make a career in the film business. The only way to break through the walls of Castle Hollywood is to find a sponsor who is *passionate* about what you've created, and such passion is normally reserved for work that is *fantastic*. So write fantastic. Your audience — and your art — deserve nothing less.

THE SECRETS

THE FOUR-ACT STRUCTURE
Hollywood's New Secret Weapon

Hollywood has traditionally viewed movies in terms of three acts. Act One, exposition, tends to occupy the first quarter of the film's running time (roughly the first thirty pages of a traditional 120-page screenplay). Act Two, story development, occupies the middle hour (pages 31-90), and Act Three, climax and resolution, takes up the final quarter (pages 91-120). Although some movies veer from this classic structure, the vast majority of commercial films continue to adhere to this paradigm. The structure has been so ingrained — and so successful — that it's the formula audiences have come to expect, and even the most brilliant and brave screenwriters don't dare violate it. The Three Act Structure is *the* language of the dramatic motion picture.

Unfortunately, most writers — veterans as well as amateurs — have problems working within this three-act framework. The phrase "problems with my second act" is so common that it's virtually a screenwriting cliché. That second act — the middle hour — is to most writers a vast, sprawling wasteland devoid of paths, landmarks, or guideposts, causing the weary traveler to stumble aimlessly for what seems an eternity until, often by sheer luck, he finally glimpses the deliverance of Act Three on the horizon and goes stumbling toward it with mad desperation.

This need not be so. There is a way to master the second act and, by doing so, to master your screenplay as a whole. The answer lies not in changing the classic structure, but in changing your *perception* of the classic structure. The solution is to think of your screen story — any screen story — in terms of *four* acts, not three. Do so and suddenly the road through the wasteland becomes clear, straight, and inviting. The Four Act Structure can, to screenwriters at any professional level, be a roadmap to success.

Here's how it works:
- Act One: The Set-Up (1-30)
- Act Two: First Quest (31-60)
- Act Three: Second Quest (61-90)
- Act Four: Climax & Resolution (91-120)

As you can see, the first and final acts retain their original positions and proportions; the middle hour, however, has been broken cleanly in half. Each new "Act" now represents an individual "quest," or goal that the story's hero is striving to attain. Following this structure, the hero begins Act Two intent on achieving Goal A. This then leads to a "mini-climax" at the mid-point, at the end of which the hero either fails and has to formulate a new goal, or succeeds, only to discover that he must accomplish another task to get The Thing He Truly Wants. This Second Quest, Act Three, then leads to the major climax, which occupies the bulk of Act Four.

The history of cinema is filled with four act movies — even though most writers didn't know they were following this paradigm. For example, there's George Lucas' *Star Wars*, the film that helped define the New Hollywood and served as a benchmark for an entire generation. In that film, we begin with young Luke Skywalker toiling way on his uncle's vapor farm until he comes into possession of two rogue 'droids, one of which carries a distress message from a captured princess, instructing them to transport the service 'droid R2D2 to her home planet of Alderaan (Act One). In Act Two, Luke attempts to fulfill the princess' request by first tracking the runaway R2D2 to Obi-Wan Kenobi, who in turn enlists the services of the mercenary smuggler Han Solo and his co-pilot, Chewbacca. As instructed, they fly R2D2 to Alderaan. But it's too late. Alderaan has just been destroyed (Act Two). Now, in Act Three, our heroes are captured by the dreaded Death Star. While in the Death Star, they rescue Princess Leia, escape with the 'droids following a fierce aerial dogfight, and deliver R2D2 to the rebel army hidden on the fourth moon of Yavin (Act Three). But the story isn't over. The Death Star has tracked them, and they must destroy the dreaded battle station before the Death Star destroys them (Act Four).

For a more recent example, let's look at *A Beautiful Mind*, 2001's Academy Award-winning screenplay by Akiva Goldsman. In that story, we begin by meeting the math prodigy John Nash, follow him as he becomes a teacher, meets his bride-to-be, and is ultimately recruited to be a government code-breaker by the mysterious Mr. Parcher (Act One.) In Act Two, we follow Nash as he woos and marries Alisha, all the while getting deeper and deeper into Cold War intrigue. Act Two climaxes with John apparently being kidnapped by Russian agents — at which point we learn that his entire "adventure" has been nothing but a schizophrenic delusion. Now, in Act Three, Nash struggles to accept the reality of his situation, taking his meds but losing his intellect and his soul in the process. He falls back into the madness, but emerges determined to fight his demons with his own mind and his own will, not drugs. Which takes us into Act Four, where we find Nash slowly but surely re-integrating himself with the academic community and his marriage even as his schizophrenic demons continue to haunt him. The story climaxes with Nash being awarded the Nobel Prize.

Examine the vast majority of successful films, both classic and contemporary, and you will find that most actually follow this four act structure. There is inevitably a major twist, reversal, or escalation at the story's mid-point (the hunter becomes the hunted, friends become lovers, the amateur masters his powers, etc.), causing the hero to change or modify his goal or otherwise take on more than he had originally intended. Second and third acts tend to be distinguished by occurring in different locations and often having very different physics or emotional dynamics. For example:

Raiders of the Lost Ark (1981) — Act Two: The Search for the Ark; Act Three: Escaping with the Ark.

Rain Man (1988) — Act Two: Charlie struggles to deal with Raymond's autism as they drive cross-country; Act Three: Charlie exploits Raymond's autism for his own gain.

Schindler's List (1993) — Act Two: Oskar Schindler exploits his Jewish laborers for his own profit; Act Three: Despite his own instincts, Schindler begins to actively protect his Jews against Nazi extermination.

Cast Away (2000) — Act Two: Having been marooned on a deserted island, Chuck Noland struggles to survive — and keep his sanity; Act Three: Four years later, Noland devises a way to escape his island prison.

THE FOUR-ACT STRUCTURE   125

Spider-man (2002) — Act Two: Peter Parker learns to master his new super-powers; Act Three: Now Spider-man, Parker battles that evil that is the Green Goblin.

Something's Gotta Give (2003) — Act Two: Harry Sanborn and Erica Barry spar as sexual adversaries; Act Three: Having slept together, Harry and Erica now must struggle with the complications of being lovers.

Obviously, there are some films — particularly those that screw with chronology like *Pulp Fiction* or *Memento*, or that are more episodic in nature that don't fit so neatly into this four act paradigm. But for anyone who simply wants to write a good-story-well-told and avoid the Second Act Doldrums, then this new approach at looking at classic story structure can be a useful way to outline your narrative, as well as better appreciate the great — and even not-so-great — works of others.

THE "WOW!" FACTOR
The Compelling Factor that Makes Your Movie Worth Making

What is it that distinguishes a screenplay that is merely well-written from one that is actually marketable? Is there a single ingredient separating scripts that producers admire from those that they actually want to *buy*? Why do some screenplays earn excellent coverage and legions of industry fans, but never go anywhere — while others of lesser quality get snapped up for millions in heated bidding wars?

The difference between screenplays that readers enjoy and those that get people to sit up and take notice can often be attributed to one thing. It's that single creative element that makes the pupils dilate, the jaw drop, and the heart pound. It's the twist, the turn, the conceit that fires the imagination and tells the audience that this project is something special. It's an elemental concept like fire, the wheel, or the number "0" that, when revealed, makes everyone slap their foreheads and shout, "Why didn't *I* think of that!"

In Hollywood, it's called the "Wow Factor."

Wow Factors can take many shapes and forms. Some are purely conceptual while others assume physical form. Some are purely intellectual while others are strongly visceral. A script's Wow Factor can be stylistic, structural, or topical. It's what gets put on the poster. It's the focus of the marketing campaign. It's the thing that grabs the public's attention and makes it say, "I have *got* to see this movie!"

A script with a Wow Factor doesn't need big stars. The Wow Factor *is* the star. Wow Factors start trends and trigger fads. They turn their movies into benchmarks against which all the films that follow are ultimately measured.

A Wow Factor may not guarantee a movie's long-term success or profitability, but it usually ensures at least a strong opening weekend. And in Hollywood, where opening night numbers are often all that stand between an executive's promotion or termination, that is more than sufficient.

Anyone writing a Hollywood screenplay — or even *thinking* about writing a Hollywood screenplay — needs to not only understand the concept of the Wow Factor, but to actively attempt to fit one into his or her project. It can mean the difference between toiling away in anonymity and unimaginable success. Wow Factors are the keys to the kingdom.

Here are the types of Wow Factors from which you can choose:

The Wow Premise: Commonly referred to as "high concept," the Wow Premise is one that is so clever, so original, and yet so simple and exciting that the movie all but "writes itself." *The Terminator* had a Wow Premise ("Killer robots from the future!") *The Ring* had a Wow Premise. ("See a haunted videotape and die in seven days!") *Bruce Almighty* had a Wow Premise ("An everyday schmuck is given divine powers!") If a Wow Premise is socially provocative enough, it can become nationwide talk show fodder (e.g. *Fatal Attraction*, *Indecent Proposal*, etc.). Even if a screenplay fails to deliver in its execution, you can sell a Wow Premise. It's the Holy Grail every screenwriter — and every studio executive — seeks.

The Wow Structure: Sometimes, it's not so much a script's story that's compelling, but *how the story is told*. Because movies are inherently temporal in nature, structure — the arrangement of narrative elements — can by itself be a compelling selling point. For example, *Pulp Fiction*, with its Mobius-strip narrative, has a Wow Structure. *Memento*, its story told in reverse order, has a Wow Structure. *Go*, with its trio of loop-de-loop plotlines, has a Wow Structure. The best Wow Structures are those that actually complement the theme of the story (e.g. *Memento*) and aren't merely cheap gimmicks. However, as cheap gimmicks go, a well-executed Wow Structure can have significant selling power.

The Wow Character: Come up with a character who is so unusual or exciting and it sometimes doesn't matter how clever the premise or how creatively structured the storyline. This often means creating a character with some extreme ability or characteristic. The autistic savant Raymond Babbit in *Rain Man* is a Wow Character. The eponymous lead in *Forrest Gump* is a Wow Character. Elle

128 SECRETS OF THE SCREEN TRADE

Woods in *Legally Blonde* is a Wow Character. The great thing about Wow Characters is that they tend to attract Wow Actors, who attract Wow Directors who attract Wow Studios and can lead to Academy Award nominations (Wow!).

The Wow SPFX: Since the dawn of cinema, special effects have been used to attract audiences by showing them places and things that simply don't exist in real life. Today, with CGI, it's even easier (and cheaper) to create fanciful locations and characters/creatures that can only be seen on the silver screen. Such effects, if well chosen, can be a screenplay's principal selling point. For example, *The Hulk*, *Godzilla*, *Jurassic Park* (and its sequels), and *Star Wars* (and its sequels and prequels) were all Wow SPFX-driven projects. Although the final box office totals on these kinds of films may vary wildly, most tend to have a high "want-to-see" factor and open strongly.

The Wow Stunt Show: Action films tend to live or die on the strength of their stunts, so the wilder and more imaginative you can make yours, the more attractive your script is going to be to both producers and audiences. Look at the trailers for *Charlie's Angels: Full Throttle*; *Lara Croft, Tomb Raider: The Cradle of Life*; *Bad Boys II*, or any James Bond film. They're not selling stories. They're not selling characters. They're selling stunts. Visceral thrills. Spectacular action — especially those involving mechanical carnage of any kind — has always been and always will be a can't-lose Wow Factor.

The Wow Taboo-Buster: Sometimes the way to get your script noticed — and a movie sold — is simply to "push the envelope" of good taste and social mores. In decades past, films like *Bonnie and Clyde*, *Don't Look Now*, *The Wild Bunch*, *Last Tango in Paris*, *Dawn of the Dead*, and *Body Heat* all challenged established boundaries for depicting sex and violence — and in doing so, set established new levels of audience acceptability. More recently, so-called "gross-out comedies" like *There's Something About Mary*, *American Pie*, and *Jackass: The Movie* have shattered comedic barriers and redefined what audiences will and will not laugh at.

Admittedly, not all movies — or even all successful movies — have the benefit of a Wow Factor. *American Beauty*, *The Hours*, *Catch Me If You Can*, and *My Big Fat Greek Wedding* are just a few recent films that did very well without obvious "Wow" elements. But if you're looking to quickly distinguish your screenplay from the others in an executive's "weekend read;" if you want to give production company readers a clear reason to recommend your movie and audiences an equally compelling reason to see it, then a Wow Factor should be a central element in your screenplay.

Bring on the killer robots!

RAISING THE DEAD
Hollywood Breathes Life into Dormant Genres

It's an old axiom that the public's taste in movies is cyclical. One year, action movies are in; the next year, they're colder than a Fargo meat locker. And it wasn't long ago that sports flicks were out — until *Remember the Titans* and *The Rookie* did huge box office. Now, once again, execs are beating the bushes for the next *Rocky*.

But while certain types of films are known to fall in and out of favor as frequently as fad diets, there are a handful of genres that Hollywood has, through the years, not only once deemed deader than Elvis, but has declared a pox on anyone who brings them up in even casual conversations.

Westerns. Musicals. Pirate movies. All of these genres were lately said to contain intrinsic sensibilities that peaked during the halcyon days of the 1950s and 1960s and have since gone into precipitous decline.

But as any horror fan from *Frankenstein* to *The Texas Chainsaw Massacre* will testify, in Hollywood, there's no such thing as "dead."

Go ahead — shoot the monster, bludgeon him, burn him, freeze him, drop him in hydrochloric acid, cut off his head, drive a stake through his heart, hurl him off a 100-foot cliff, and then shove a 5,000-pound bunker-buster up his ass for good measure. But if box office figures soar, you can bet the farm that the SOB will be back for more abuse sooner than you can say *I Still Know What You Did Last Summer*.

And so it has been in Hollywood lately with genres that had previously looked about as viable as a blintz stand in Baghdad.

Take westerns, which have been on Hollywood's Honorary Dead List since the Ford Administration. The genre was the cinematic equivalent of the California Mother Lode, a vein once bursting with seemingly unending riches, but mined with such speed and frenzy that only occasional flecks of beauty remain.

Cowboys and Indians were once so dominant that an entire Emmy category was devoted to them, but recent attempts to revive the genre range from tepid (e.g., Tom Berenger's *Peacemakers*) to disastrous (the recent *The Lone Ranger* MOW). Today, there is a glint to be found in HBO's *Deadwood*, which has proven to be a critical darling and may well pave the way for yet another resurgence of the genre.

Musicals — traditional entertainments where songs are an integral part of the actual storyline — are also in the midst of a surprising comeback. For more than two decades, these films in which orchestral music swells impromptu and characters spontaneously break into glorious song and dance, seemed increasingly hokey. Save for Disney animated features such as *The Little Mermaid, Beauty & The Beast*, and *The Lion King*, live action movie musicals have been held in such ill-favor that you had to go all the way back to 1972 to find a genre specimen nominated for Best Picture (*Cabaret*).

All that changed in 2001 with *Moulin Rouge* when helmer Baz Luhrmann fused classic twentieth century pop songs with MTV-style techniques while turning Ewan McGregor and Nicole Kidman into a modern-day version of Astaire and Rodgers. The film scored well with critics, achieved sensational box office returns, and went on to receive eight Academy Award nominations, including one for Best Picture.

A year later, Miramax's *Chicago*, a more traditional musical, hit pay dirt ($306 million worldwide), and walked away with six Oscars, including Best Picture. To try to mimic the achievement, Miramax is planning remakes of *Guys & Dolls* and *Bye, Bye Birdie*. One can only wonder if *Fiddler on the Roof* will be next.

Of all the dormant genres now being brought back to life, none have seemed a less likely candidate for resurrection than the pirate movie. This category peaked in the late 1940s and early 1950s with such films as *Treasure Island* and *The Crimson Pirate*. Since then, every decade or so some brave soul has attempted to raise the Jolly Roger again, but generally with disastrous results.

In 1976, Robert Shaw wasted all the goodwill he'd earned with *Jaws* in the utterly painful *Swashbuckler*. Ten years later, movie houses nationwide were plagued with a Gilbert-and-Sullivan meets *The Blue Lagoon* embarrassment, *The Pirate Movie*, as well as Roman Polanski's dog, *Pirates*. And who can forget Renny Harlin's immortal *Cutthroat Island*, the 1995 mega-bomb that helped sink Carolco?

Based on this consistent string of flops, it would stand to reason that studios would be afraid to get back in the water. Not so, thanks to Disney, who bravely released *Pirates of the Caribbean*, a movie based on its famous theme park ride. Surprisingly, *Pirates* became the number-one live action film of the year, in no small part due to the casting of Johnny Depp as a charming Keith Richards-inspired ne'er-do-well.

How has Hollywood managed to revive the dead? Is it just a matter of dumb luck that westerns, musicals, and pirates have each managed to ascend from the grave at approximately the same time, or is it the current zeitgeist that has caused audiences worldwide to suddenly embrace them? Could it also be that mainstream filmmakers have discovered a way to breathe new life into these previously dead categories?

For filmmakers considering taking a fresh shot at genres once considered out, the following guidelines might be of some help:

Keep it period. In times of war and bad economies, audiences are famous for wanting to escape into other times and places. Westerns and pirate movies (as well as WW II films and sword-and-sandal epics — other genres that have been recently resurrected) are usually set in distant time periods and naturally offer a clean retreat from current circumstances. The success of *Chicago*, for instance, could be due in large part to its period setting. If you buy that logic, then prospects for *Guys & Dolls* and *Bye, Bye Birdie* are promising.

Cast iconic actors. Genre movies are, by definition, iconic. They stand as symbols for a host of concepts, themes, and moral systems that have accumulated around them over time. Giving such stories maximum power and weight requires the casting of huge, much-loved actors. *Saving Private Ryan* was helped immeasurably by the presence of Tom Hanks, who is about as All-American as the Statue of Liberty, while Johnny Depp — the modern personification of eccentricity — brought a degree of deranged dignity to *Pirates of the Caribbean*.

Embrace modern filmmaking technology. Just because a film is based on an old genre doesn't mean it has to *look* old. *Moulin Rouge* and *Chicago* used sweeping camera moves and rapid-fire editing embraced by hip generations. *Pirates of the Caribbean, Gladiator, Master and Commander,* and *Saving Private Ryan* all employed advanced CGI effects that put past genre efforts to shame.

Never forget: Story is still king. Nothing kills a genre film faster than a bad story. And nothing can revive an out of fashion genre faster than a good yarn. All of the recent films mentioned here were blessed with strong screenplays that used well-drawn characters and complex plots to explore intriguing themes. They were put in the hands of directors who embraced their respective genres and didn't attempt to undercut them. The stories were taken seriously — or, as in the case of *Pirates of the Caribbean*, with a *Raiders*-like sense of fun — and the result was a set of movies that any filmmaker would be proud to have in his portfolio.

If these first years of the 21st century have taught us anything, it's that no genre is ever completely washed up. Given the proper subject, story, cast, and approach, even the most seemingly irrelevant genre can be a contender for Mr. Moviefone's Top Five list.

So it appears now that only a lack of imagination or simple courage would prompt a studio executive to dismiss a project simply because its genre is out of vogue.

Which begs the question — how long will it be until we see *Tarzan, The Musical?*

BLIND TURNS
Avoiding the Predictable Screen Story

One of the most common criticisms that professional story analysts and studio executives level against spec scripts is that they're "predictable." By this they mean that, very early in the story's development the audience has enough information to determine not only how the story will end, but how it will get there.

While the problem of predictability is simple to understand, it can be extremely difficult to overcome. After all, how many choices does a writer really have? Either the hero wins or the hero loses — and if this is a Hollywood movie, it's a good bet that the hero's going to win, period. The underdog *has* to win the big game at the last possible second; the ugly duckling *has* to win the hand of the handsome prince; Spider-man *has* to defeat Doc Ock. Watching the hero win is why we go to the movies in the first place.

It can also be argued that predictability isn't really as big a problem as the use of this criticism might suggest. After all, knowing in advance that Jesus was going to die and be resurrected didn't hurt the grosses of *The Passion of the Christ*. Knowing that the boat sinks didn't keep *Titanic* from being the top-grossing moving of all time. And what about repeat viewers? They know the whole damned movie already and they *still* pay to see it again! (Don't lie: How many times have *you* watched that *Raiders of the Lost Ark* DVD?)

Good arguments, all — and completely irrelevant when it comes to avoiding predictability. When we go to a movie, we know that the story has been contrived to satisfy us, yet we want to believe that what unfolds is doing so for the first time. It's like watching a good professional magician at work; we know he's performing illusions, but we want to believe in miracles.

As a writer, you become that magician, and you achieve your illusions the way magicians do — through the elegant art of misdirection. Here, then, are some tricks — er, *techniques* — that you can use to keep your audience guessing:

Escalate at the midpoint. The traditional, "linear" way to tell a story is to give your hero a goal at the end of Act One, and then have him or her achieve that goal at the end of Act Three. There will usually be obstacles along the way, yes, but ultimately you arrive at the point you promised the audience some ninety minutes earlier.

A better way to weave your tale is to have your hero reach the intended goal not at the end of the end of the story, but at the *midpoint* (or thereabouts). Then twist this seeming triumph by having the hero discover that he has only achieved *part* of what he or she really wants/needs, and that far more work is necessary before the story can be brought to a true close. The stakes have been raised. The story has "escalated."

A classic example of this is 1964's *Goldfinger*, arguably the best of all the twenty or so James Bond pictures and the one that set the template for all Bond films to follow. In that scenario, Bond is initially dispatched by British Intelligence to learn how multi-millionaire Auric Goldfinger is smuggling gold bullion out of Europe. Only *after* the film's midpoint does Bond learn that Goldfinger's real plan is to blow up Fort Knox with an atomic bomb. If Bond's mission had been to stop the Fort Knox bombing from the onset, the film would have been far more predictable — and significantly less interesting.

Withhold information from your hero. A great way to hold your audience's interest is to keep your hero — and therefore audience — in the dark about key information for as long as possible. Everyone loves a mystery, and as long as the audience and its dramatic surrogate, the hero, are both asking "What the hell is going on?", interest will be held and predictability avoided. Thousands of thrillers, from *Gaslight* to *Minority Report*, have succeeded by employing this technique.

Withhold information from your audience. An excellent way to stay ahead of your audience is to simply have your hero (or other characters) act on information they've received but that the audience has not. If your audience is consistently asking itself, "What...?", then predictability is prevented. Most caper and con films employ this technique. Watch *The Sting* or *Ocean's Eleven* (either version) to see how the writers succeed admirably just by keeping their narrative cards close to the vest. They give us only as much information as we need to *think* we understand what's going on, revealing key information at the last possible moment to create a satisfying climax and conclusion.

Lie to your hero. In any investigative story, the hero spends most of his or her time trying to discover and process information. The audience is kept guessing along with the lead character. However, it can be even more effective to have other characters deliberately *lie* to the hero — and thus the audience — allowing the hero to be sent in wrong directions or led to make destructive decisions. There are any number of reasons characters lie; perhaps they're trying to protect themselves, protect someone else, or simply further their own agendas. Any story in which a seeming ally is revealed to be an enemy agent (e.g. Cypher in *The Matrix*) is employing this classic but always effective diversion.

Weaken your hero. Because we can safely bet that a hero is going to triumph, you should continuously weaken your hero to the point that victory seems impossible and unobtainable. Such weakening can be done, physically, mentally, financially, socially, or emotionally, and can be either the result of random circumstance or direct action by the antagonist (or agents thereof). Even while your audience may remain confident that virtue will triumph in the end, you can build tension by prompting viewers to ask themselves "*How will virtue triumph?*" To pull this off successfully, you must have already planted somewhere in your script the means by which your hero can emerge victorious (*without* resorting to incredible or *deus ex machina*-style contrivances).

The big "reveal": One way to really screw with an audience's mind is stage a massive "reveal" in Act III that completely reorients their perspective on the events that have previously transpired. More than a simple "twist" ending, this kind of "reveal" completely redefines the story by telling the audience that the story they thought they were was seeing was not the actual story at all. Sometimes the characters in "big reveal" stories discover, or are otherwise made aware of, this critical new information; sometimes they are not. However, to make such a story satisfying, you have to make damned sure that the narrative holds up on repeat viewings by people who now know your "secret" and know what "clues" to look for along the way.

Recent examples of such stories include *The Sixth Sense*, *The Others*, *Fight Club*, *Memento*, *Vanilla Sky*, *Identity*, and *The Secret Window*.

But be careful. "It's all just a dream," "He's a schizophrenic," and, "She's really dead," are, at this point, such clichéd reveals that a seasoned movie-goer can spot them a mile away.

To review: predictability is a problem all writers must deal with, and among the ways to overcome this challenge is to deliberately withhold information, misdirect, or outright lie to your hero and/or audience to keep everyone guessing — and interested.

Or you can just end with having everyone hit by a bus.

See, I'll bet you didn't see *that* coming, did you?

DON'T LOOK IN THE BASEMENT
And Other Tricks for Building Cinematic Suspense

There's a classic and highly instructive scene in 2002's sci-fi/suspense hit *Signs*, written and directed by M. Night Shyamalan, when former preacher Graham Hess (Mel Gibson) has just been told by his very nervous neighbor Ray Reddy (Shyamalan again) that Reddy has trapped an alien invader in his kitchen pantry. Compelled to investigate this fantastic claim, Hess ventures into the Reddy house where, indeed, *something* is moving behind the barricaded pantry door. Step by tentative step, Hess approaches the mystery door, his hand visibly quivering as he reaches for the doorknob. What's on the other side? An animal? An unjustly imprisoned vagrant? Or perhaps — just perhaps — it is the true stuff of nightmares. In the theater, not a soul in the packed house dare breathes in maddening anticipation of whatever it is Hess is about to reveal.

Now let's flashback a year to David Lynch's *Mulholland Drive*. In one of many memorable scenes, two friends sit in a classic Hollywood-area diner discussing one of the characters' recurring dreams. In this dream, these same two men are sitting in this very same diner discussing, well, dreams. Then they venture outside to the rear parking lot. Behind a wall they encounter a hideous monster. Skeptical, the listener insists that they go to the parking lot to see if the dream was, in fact, a premonition. The two friends go to the rear parking lot and, indeed, there is the very wall the other man had seen in his night vision. Slowly, they approach the barricade. They hesitate. Then they press forward. What's on the other side? Will there be nothing but an overflowing dumpster — or perhaps —

just perhaps — a hideous monster will leap from the shadows and devour them both!

Both of these scenes are extremely effective examples of classic cinematic suspense. Using the simplest of low-tech techniques, they capture and hold their audience's attention in ways many multi-million-dollar action set-pieces can only envy. Say what you will about Shamalyan's over-use of narrative contrivance or Lynch's contempt for coherent structure, both *Signs* and *Mulholland Drive* have moments that positively transfix the viewer and prompt the million-dollar question: What's going to happen next?

Understanding how to create and build suspense and then using these techniques artfully can often spell the difference between a movie that is merely interesting and one with true audience impact.

Here then are the most common — and effective — methods that filmmakers from Hitchcock onward have used to promote an oh-so-splendid sense of anticipatory dread. Use them at your own risk:

Don't look in the basement! This is the sure-fire technique used in the two scenes described above as well as countless of cheapo horror films. Like so many dramatic set-ups, it involves a warning that must inevitably be ignored. However, unlike the typical admonishment that carries with it a specific consequence, the threat here is of the unknown (which, as we all know, is far more terrifying than anything corporeal). While the specifics may vary from story to story, the set-up always goes something like, "Behind that door is the most gruesome, most awful thing you will ever see in your life. For the love of God, whatever you do, don't open that door!" How can any red-blooded screen character resist a challenge like that? And how can an attentive audience react to the sight of the tentative hand reaching for the doorknob except by clinging to the edges of their collective seats? (For another wonderful example of this technique at work, check out the "What's Under the Dinner Plate Cover?" scene in Robert Aldrich's 1962 camp classic, *What Ever Happened to Baby Jane?*)

I know something you don't know. Also known as the "Oblivious Hero Ruse," it involves showing the audience a source of danger of which the on-screen hero remains blissfully unaware. Classic sources of unseen danger include hidden bombs (usually ticking), failing structural supports (usually termite-ridden), and lurking killers (always armed). Kevin Williamson's *Scream* movies both exploited and parodied this always-effective technique by frequently putting their protagonists in the foreground while the costumed assassin flitted about unnoticed behind them. Audiences worldwide were white-knuckled with giddy panic during these sequences, often shouting aloud for the heroes to "Turn the fuck around!" while simultaneously wondering why serial-killer victims appear to universally lack any sort of peripheral vision.

Beat the clock. "Ticking Clock" is the industry term for any time limit required to complete a particular goal. Ticking clocks are often used to give entire movies form and dramatic tension. ("He has just two days to find a bride or lose a billion-dollar inheritance!) However, as film is a temporal medium, literal "ticking clocks" are excellent devices for significantly heightening suspense in individual scenes — especially when those clocks are tied to irreversible events (e.g., airplanes taking off, games ending, bombs exploding, etc). Time being a tyrant we all fear, requiring a character to travel vast distances or overcome seemingly insurmountable obstacles while a clock ticks down toward 00:00 has become an always-reliable way to increase audience anxiety in everything from sports pictures to action films to romantic comedies.

When time stands still. The flipside of the "Beat the Clock" technique is "When Time Stands Still," deliberately slowing down the perceived passage of time to milk suspense for all it's worth. A primary practitioner of this art form is Brian De Palma. In many of his films, from *Carrie* and *Obsession* to *Dressed to Kill*, De Palma will slow the action, stretching out moments for the specific purpose of heightening audience anxiety. However, unlike "Beat the Clock," this suspense tool is very delicate. For as any De Palma devotee will attest, there is a very fine line between anxiety and boredom.

The cliffhanger. Taking its name from the act of having a hero literally dangle from a cliff's edge during the climax of many an early silent movie, the "Cliffhanger" relies on one's ability to create a credibly high degree of physical danger — usually involving heights — while simultaneously concocting an equally credible escape route. Perhaps the best execution of the "Cliffhanger" technique achieved in the past decade was in, appropriate enough, 1993's *Cliffhanger*. The opening sequence, which found mountaineer Stallone trying to rescue a damsel-in-distress suspended hundreds of feet above a rocky canyon was a brilliantly successful exercise in jaw-clenching, nail-biting, knee-weakening, nausea-inducing acrophobic terror. For other classic "Cliffhangers," check out the climaxes to *Blade*

Runner, *Indiana Jones & The Temple of Doom*, *True Lies*, and the gold standard — the opening sequence of Hitchock's *Vertigo*.

The lady or the tiger. So named for Frank Stockton's classic tale of ambiguity, this might also be called "The Red Wire/Green Wire Conundrum." In such a sequence, a character is confronted with an either/or decision. One choice will result in victory, pleasure, safety, riches, and/or world peace. The other choice inevitably leads to quick and painful death (or its dramatic equivalent). And just to complicate matters, there's no logical way to determine the correct course of action. Ultimately, the hero has to take a leap of faith. If it's the first act, the character's choice is inevitably the wrong one and — KA-BLAM. (Needless to say, the "Lady or the Tiger" choice is rarely given to A-List actors in the first thirty pages of a screenplay.) In Act Three, the "blind choice" usually turns out to be the correct one, and everyone goes home happy. A cliché? Of course. And dang it if it doesn't work every time.

Like all classic dramatic devices, it's important to use these tools sparingly and, one hopes, with enough originality and panache to rise above predictable convention. However, like really good chocolate or excellent coffee, these time-tested techniques never fail to satisfy.

Now, if you'll excuse us, there's something scratching at our back door and we're just *dying* to see what it is...

HOLLYWOOD JACKASS
The Masochist's Guide to Studio Screenwriting

In *Jackass: The Movie*, the big-screen version of the gleefully irresponsible MTV "reality" show, Johnny Knoxville and his band of merry masochists hurl themselves into walls, have baby alligators bite their nipples, and otherwise subject themselves to all manner of physical abuse for the amusement of blood-lusting audiences everywhere. Attracting hoards of iconoclastic teenage males who would no doubt have felt right at home in the stands of the Roman Coliseum, *Jackass: The Movie* went on to become one of the most profitable films of late 2002.

But why should people who recklessly drive golf carts through miniature golf courses have all the fun? Since movies like *Jackass* and unscripted TV shows have put legions of screenwriters out of work, is there a way for danger-loving dramatists to show their mettle by facing death — and living to tell the tale?

Here, for your consideration, are some "extreme" screenwriting stunts guaranteed to horrify and outrage studio readers and executives alike, and earn you the coveted title of "Hollywood Jackass":

The casting coach. For writers eager to lead with their proverbial chins, nothing says, "Hate Me," quite so elegantly as placing casting choices in character introductions. Those new to the game are advised to take the tried-and-true route of suggesting established A-List $20-million-a-picture-not-available-until-September-2008 actors like Brad Pitt, Julia Roberts, Harrison Ford, or Tom Cruise, while the slightly more experienced masochist may prefer to insist on "hot young stars" like Scarlett Johansson or Jake Gyllenhaal for their lead roles. For those truly daring, suggesting obscure or no-name indie actors can make you look daring and moronic at the same time, while the totally fearless will go for broke and suggest actors who are *dead*. "Think Steve McQueen..." "Think Marilyn Monroe..." Think *idiot*...!

The endless opus. Anyone can infuriate a reader with molasses-thick description, broken English, or just plain bad grammar. But to put a reader in a homicidal mood before he or she even gets past the title page takes extra effort — and lots of extra paper. Novices are advised to start easy by submitting scripts weighing in at hardy 130 or 135 pages (for extra points, use a really small font and narrow margins). Once yours bruises heal, it's time to get serious with a 150-to-180-page "epic." Hey, James Cameron movies run three hours, why can't yours? Want to be a true Master of Disaster? Throw all caution — and common sense — to the wind and send readers a five-part TV miniseries! Remember, readers get paid the same flat fee regardless of a script's length, so the more you can reduce their dollar-per-page average, the more ire-per-page you generate in return!

Hey, is this thing on...? Some say that nothing is quite so loud as a whisper. BULLSHIT!!! says the Hollywood Jackass. We all know that to call attention to IMPORTANT OBJECTS in a screenplay or to help actors EMPHASIZE THEIR WORDS, we need to PUT WORDS IN REALLY BIG TYPE! With LOTS OF EXCLAMATION POINTS!!!!! TO MAKE SURE READERS PAY ATTENTION!!! And what's IMPORTANT in your screenplay? Why, EVERYTHING, OF COURSE!!! That's why there are SO MANY UPPERCASED WORDS and UPPERCASED DIALOGUE in your REALLY EXCITING SCREENPLAY!!!! (Please excuse me while I get a Tylenol....)

The unsolicited sequel. Nothing says "brazen idiot" quite like submitting an unsolicited sequel to a successful film to which you own no legal rights whatsoever. Sending *Spider-man II* or *The Ring Returns* over the transom is an act of foolhardy courage guaranteed to have D-girls giggling behind your back for days. For extra points, write an installment of a well-established franchise like *Star Wars* or James Bond, and attach a note saying, "The last movie *sucked. This* is the movie you *should* have made." Why, it's more fun than jumping naked onto a barrel cactus!

Everything you ever wanted to know about Joe, and never cared to ask. That giant gnashing sound you regularly hear from Hollywood is the sound of thousands of jaws clenching every time a character introduction is accompanied by a paragraph-long biography. Yes, when Joe enters the room, it's really important for readers to know that "He was born poor but has struggled to educate himself and through hard work and discipline managed to turn a struggling computer software company into the world's largest supplier of network routers." How about we just cut to the part where you fearlessly dig your own eye out with a fork?

Say *what*? Back in the 1960s, author Anthony Burgess gained literary notoriety by combining elements of English, Cockney, and Russian to create a unique future slang for his book *A Clockwork Orange*. Show your own literary pretense — as well as your own total lack of market savvy — by writing a science-fiction, fantasy or mythological screen story filled with unpronounceable names, undecipherable proto-dialogue and exhausting technobabble. Remember, paid readers don't have the luxury of being able to just throw your script away after ten pages, even if it makes no sense. They have to read the *whole thing!* And *write a synopsis!* That *does* make sense! True masters at this extreme game have been known to reduce even experienced readers to tears by the end of Act One and send them begging for jobs in the insurance business.

You talkin' to *me*? Readers are a lonely lot. They spend their working hours alone in dark little rooms staring at endless words on equally endless sheets of paper with little or no human contact. So why not drive them *totally* crazy by filling your screenplay with incessant first-person commentary, presumptuous rhetorical questions and annoying entreaties that repeatedly shatter any sense of reality you may have inadvertently created? After all, what does a lonely reader want more than some unknown hack who insists on desperately engaging them in disembodied one-way conversation? Hey, I'm talkin' to *you*!

Slice of life. Just as any untalented boob can skateboard into a garage door, any jerk with an e-Machine and a pirated copy of Final Draft can accomplish the stunts described above (and many already have!). It takes a true artist — preferably one with an extreme death wish — to pull off this last insidious gambit. It involves writing a perfectly formatted, technically unimpeachable screenplay — usually a drama, and often in a period setting — which at first *appears* to be a work of a legitimate writer, but which...ever-so-slowly and with painful precision...reveals itself to be about — *nothing!* People talk and talk but say nothing. They act but accomplish nothing. There are no goals. No conflicts. No action. No humor. Yes, it's a "Slice of Life!" It was Alfred Hitchcock who once described movies as "life with all the boring parts taken out." The champion Hollywood Jackass takes all the boring parts discarded by other writers and assembles them into their own "I've just wasted two hours of my life I'm never getting back" theft of a reader's soul.

Remember, all of the stunts listed above are for professionals only. Do not try them at home.

STOP ME IF YOU'VE HEARD THIS ONE
Ten Movie Premises to Avoid

Everyone in Hollywood knows the value of a good story concept. Yes, good dialogue can bring life and energy to a screenplay, but its actual market value is so low that the Writers Guild doesn't even consider dialogue a factor when determining screenplay credits. Structure is certainly critical to a movie's effectiveness, but structure can be changed in the editing room as easily as on the word processor, and so doesn't play a primary role in a screenplay's sales potential. Attractive, sympathetic characters, heart-pounding action sequences, gut-busting humor, hot sex, and dazzling special effects all add undeniable value to a motion picture property, but all of these elements can be added at any point in the development process by any number of capable writers.

No, in the end, premise and premise alone is the one unique element that you, the screenwriter, can bring to the table that no one else can duplicate. Come up with a dramatically powerful or irresistibly hilarious idea, and your path to success — while never guaranteed — will certainly contain far fewer obstacles than you might have otherwise encountered.

Unfortunately, one person's definition of an "original premise" is too often another person's cliché. People who read and recommend scripts for producers and studios will tell you that there are a number premises that their authors are convinced are "original," yet are actually so common that when the logline appears, they're ready to reject the script even before they turn to the first page.

Some of these cliché premises have achieved that ignominious status because the concept has already been used and then re-used in countless motion picture treatments (e.g. serial killers, body-switches, stalkers). Others story concepts have never actually been realized on the silver screen, but the same premise keeps showing up in spec after spec to the point where readers *think* they've seen the movie even if they haven't.

Here are ten examples of movies that have been written over and over with only minor variations:

The cure for cancer: A paranoid thriller about a dedicated medical researcher who discovers the cure for cancer, only to be hunted down by ruthless agents of the medical/pharmaceutical complex who have billions invested in ongoing research and treatment. Inevitably, this story is pursued by someone who has never actually been in the medical profession and attempts to exploit the public's perceived cynicism toward both doctors and big business.

The family reunion: A low-concept drama about estranged siblings who gather for a family event — usually a funeral — and after much yelling, screaming, and crying, they all manage to work out their differences. Far too often, this story is used as a form of therapy by the writers themselves and lacks the kind of genuine entertainment value that would make it a marketable commercial film project.

Cursed ground: A family moves into a remote house only to find it inhabited by the restless spirits of a mass murder/Indian massacre/Civil War battle/etc. The "cursed ground" premise worked well for *Poltergeist* and *The Amityville Horror*, but those films are twenty-five years old. Today's audiences have seen these films so many times that they're now inevitably pages ahead of the characters.

Beat the house: A bunch of computer geeks use various technological tricks to rip off a Vegas casino. "Beating the house" is a universal fantasy, but watching other people gamble is usually about as exciting as watching someone else play a videogame. The bottom line is, gambling is not a spectator's sport. It's even less exciting when the players cheat.

The Jesus clone: A blood sample from the Shroud of Turin is cloned into a modern-day Jesus Christ — testing the faith of the Christian world. When cloning became popularly understood in the late 1980s and early 1990s, dozens of writers simultaneously stumbled onto the obvious idea of cloning Jesus. And they're still doing it. Unfortunately, films about religious faith — as opposed to classic religious stories like *The Ten Commandments* or *The Passion of the Christ* — inevitably get murky, and few writers have ever found a way to satisfactorily pay off this premise.

The Jesus body: In this variation on the Jesus Clone, archeologists find the actual body of Jesus Christ — again testing the faith of the Christian world. See above for why this story has yet to be filmed.

The fulfilled woman: A woman — young or old, singled, married, divorced, or widowed — goes off in search of personal fulfillment. This idea of female "self-realization" was fresh and compelling when Jill Clayburgh did *An Unmarried Woman* back in 1978. Twenty-five years later, the story feels like it's twenty-five years old. Enough modern women are succeeding on their own that to advance the theory that a woman can, in fact, be independent is today merely stating the obvious.

Prime suspect: A detective investigates a murder, only to discover that the leading suspect is — gasp! — himself! Kevin Costner did it in 1987's *No Way Out* (as did Ray Milland in the first version of this story, 1948's *The Big Clock*). Denzel Washington did it in *Out of Time*. We don't need to do it again.

Erich Von Daniken lives! Archeologists discover that an ancient monument was actually built by — gasp — aliens! This story is usually mixed with elements of reincarnation, alternate realities, and ESP to create a New Age stew that goes down as smoothly as pureed wheat grass. These stories usually fail because, (1) they try to cram too many fantastic ideas into a single story, and (2) they presume that everyone in the audience shares the same mystical, starry-eyed *Dungeons & Dragons*-meets-*We-Are-the-World* philosophy. The only way to pull something like this off is with a twisted sense of humor, á la *Men in Black*. And that's already been done.

Hollywood screenwriter makes it big! The ultimate wish-fulfillment fantasy of being a successful Hollywood screenwriter, which tends to bear little if any resemble to actual screenwriting (e.g., the hero becomes famous). Writing about writing is the absolute worst form of artistic self-indulgence and should be avoided at all costs.

If you recognize any of these plots as your own, don't despair. You've been warned early enough so that you can put your screenplay aside and start developing a premise that is, in fact, truly original.

Like the one about the serial killer and the cop *who are really the same person....!*

"AT LAST HE UNDERSTANDS..."
And Other Crimes of the Amateur Screenwriter

"Nick sees the photo of Gray and Shirley on the fireplace mantel-piece. At last he understands the shocking truth — his brother and his girlfriend have been setting him up!"

On its face, this simple piece of narrative prose seems innocuous enough. It describes a revelation, a moment when a character puts together a series of clues and experiences a dramatic epiphany. You'll find this kind of description in any number of novels, short stories, and even dramatic story treatments. Some may call it good writing, some may call it bad writing. But one thing is for certain: It's *not* screenwriting.

You might find this statement puzzling. No doubt you've read similar passages in any number of spec screenplays. You may have even written just such a scene in one of our own scripts. If you have indeed committed such words to paper, then you are personally responsible for your screenplay being thrown across a room some-where in Hollywood. Because while such description is perfectly acceptable in the world of narrative fiction, motion picture industry story analysts, development executives, producers, directors, and virtually all other Hollywood professionals know that there's no way for such an "understanding" — a purely interior mental process — to be conveyed on the screen.

Hence, it's not screenwriting.

It's been said that screenwriting is the toughest form of fiction. And that's probably true. It's certainly the most restrictive. Unlike novelists, who can employ any number of literary devices to communicate with their audiences — devices that include limitless description, first-, second- and third-person voices, interior monologues, commentary, asides, and even footnotes — the screenwriter is limited to just four instruments: action, dialogue, sound, and imagery. That's it. Nothing more. And with good reason. That's all the information film is able to convey.

When you see a movie, you are not privy to the characters' innermost thoughts or feelings, only those words and behaviors the actor actually performs. When you see an object or location, you cannot know the history and background of what you're seeing unless such information is conveyed either through dialogue or a visual device such as a title card. And when a character performs an action, you cannot know *why* it's being done unless the previous action provides obvious justification or the character stops to offer a verbal explanation (which may or may not be the truth).

Learning to write cinematically is key to becoming an effective screenwriter. It's also key to being recognized as a professional-level screenwriter by industry pros who are trained to recognize the difference.

Following are some of the common errors made by amateur screenwriters and ways to achieve the same ends through more "cinematic" techniques:

The revelation: This often takes the form of "He understands…", "She realizes…", "He recognizes…" or even a non-personalized, but still unacceptable declaration like "Jack is the real killer!" These and any other "interior" descriptions are to be avoided at all costs. (As is often noted by screenplay critics: Audiences cannot read a character's mind. Not in good films, at least.) The "cinematic" way to convey this kind of epiphany is to either insert a series of quick flashbacks that focus on key visuals and allow the reader/audience to put the information together on their own, to have the character convey this revelation through dialogue or, best of all, to simply have your images and actions speak for themselves.

The explanation: This is where the screenwriter speaks directly to the reader to provide information necessary to understand a situation or a character's behavior. It's not uncommon for readers to encounter description such as, "As required by German law, Anna wears a yellow armband emblazoned with a six-pointed Star of David that identifies her as a Jew," or, "Terrified of water ever since he was a boy, Nick just stands helplessly as the river's edge while he watches Susan fight a losing battle against the raging current." Obviously, an audience wouldn't have access to these writers' explanations, so why include them in a screenplay? In the first case, less is clearly more: "Anna wears a yellow armband emblazoned with a Star of David." The well-known image conveys everything the audience needs to know. In the second case, giving the actor an emotion to *play* helps provide the necessary background: "Nick approaches the water's edge. Fear floods his face. His body tenses. Clearly terrified, he stands helplessly at the river's edge while he watches Susan fight a losing battle against the raging current." That Nick has been "terrified of the water ever since he was a boy" is information that could at some point come out in dialogue; here, however, all we need to *see* is that he's afraid of water *now*.

The biography: When characters first appear, some writers feel obligated to provide a short biography, e.g., "Louis is in his mid-20s. Born into wealth and a product of the East Coast's finest private schools, he carries himself with a sense of confidence and entitlement that borders on arrogance." Although we can *see* that this character is "in his mid 20s," there's no way that we can *see* that he was "born into wealth" and is "a product of the East Coast's finest private schools." Therefore, a more cinematic description might read, "Louis is in his mid-20s. He carries himself with a sense of confidence, entitlement — even arrogance — that suggests an upper-class upbringing." They key word here is "suggests." An audience will be able to see this character's *demeanor* and hear the way he *speaks*, and a talented actor can certainly imbue these behaviors with the characteristics associated with East Coast Brahmins. Whether or not he's actually upper-class — or if, like Patricia Highsmith's Thomas Ripley, he's merely a pretender — is information that will have to come out in the body of the story.

The aside: This is where the screenwriter speaks directly to the reader and offers commentary on the action, for example, "Michael, like all the members of his clan, is deviously charming. He is not to be trusted." "Charming" is certainly a behavior an actor can play. However, "like all members of his clan" is a generalization than cannot be supported unless we are allowed to see *all* the members of his extended family — which is probably not what the author intends. And "He is not to be trusted"? That is a conclusion the audience must be allowed to draw for itself on the basis of what subsequently occurs.

The footnote: Although rarer than the errors described above, this no-no appears often enough to warrant an official warning. Usually associated with obscure or foreign words and/or references — and often cropping up in dialogue — the "footnote" can take the form of a parenthetical (e.g. "Crossing the *taiga* [boreal forest] could take weeks!"), or even a literal footnote (e.g. "Crossing the *taiga***** could take weeks!" [* Boreal forest.]). The solution here is to either avoid the foreign word or phrase altogether, substituting one that is better known to general audiences, or to use it frequently enough or in conjunction with a visual reference so that its meaning ultimately becomes clear.

Like Japanese haiku, screenwriting is a highly restrictive art form that nonetheless offers innumerable possibilities to those who can master it. Restricting one's self to imagery, dialogue, action, and sound may sound confining, but as any successful — and well-paid — professional screenwriter knows, these building blocks of cinema can be combined in infinite combinations to create virtual worlds of infinite power and complexity.

RED FLAGS
Formatting Errors that Drive Readers Crazy

They say you can't judge a book by its cover. But a screenplay is a different story. If the cover is illustrated, emblazoned with fancy type fonts, or day-glo orange, chances are the script inside will be a stinker.

At least that's the consensus among the half dozen professional script analysts and development executives we spoke with about the formatting "red flags" that usually alert them to an amateur or otherwise sub-professional submission.

"Nine times out of ten, creative formatting gimmicks are just an excuse to disguise a weak story," says story analyst and screenwriter Michael Givens, who has been evaluating scripts for over a dozen years for such producers as Joe Wizan, Dale Rosenbloom, and Cinemaline Films. "When I see an illustrated cover, I always know I'm in trouble."

All of the professionals interviewed agreed that formatting, while hardly the end all of good screenwriting, is the first step to winning a reader's favor. And with over 30,000 screenplays registered annually with the Writers Guild of America, it's critical for screenwriters to do everything they can do to get their work taken seriously.

In addition to fancy covers, here are some of the classic "red flags" that alert these decision-makers to sub-par material, and ways to help you avoid them:

Scripts are too long or short. "If I have a lot of reading to do, and I get a script that's over 130 pages long, it goes straight to the bottom of the pile," says Larry Hymes, formerly the senior vice president of development for Chanticleer Films.

"Our company guidelines for scripts is a maximum of 120 pages," agreed Carolyn Manetti, vice president of production for Maple Shade Productions. "And anything less that 100 is probably too thin."

Improper type fonts. Before the advent of word processors, screenplays were manually typed in "Pica" typeface. Today, that style otherwise known as 12-point Courier (10 cpi) — remains the industry standard. Unfortunately, too many amateurs try using different fonts to "distinguish" themselves. And some really go overboard to their disadvantage.

"The worst script I ever read was one in which the writer used a different font for every character, every action verb, and every location," Givens says. "I mean, there must have been fifty different fonts on each page. Obviously, the writer was trying to be clever, but the script was absolutely maddening. After about thirty pages, I actually turned it back to my boss and said, 'Sorry, I can't read this.'"

Improper binding. Professional screenplays are always three-hole punched and fastened with brass brads in the top and bottom holes.

"As trivial as it sounds, when a script is submitted with three brads instead of the usual two, I always know it's coming from someone who doesn't know what he's doing," says Steve Hollecker, once a creative executive for producer Lloyd Segan.

Overwritten pages. "Title pages should contain your title, your name, and contact information. Nothing more," Hymes advised. "Above all, don't date your script. You never want a producer to think your script is old."

Improper/Incomplete scene slugs. "I want to know if a scene is an interior or an exterior, and what time of day it's taking place," says Jody Paul, who has been evaluating screenplays for more than five years and currently reads for UTA. "If I don't have this simple information, I'm confused."

Typographical errors. "I hate typos," Manetti says. "I find them very annoying. Always proofread your screenplay several times, and then have a friend do it, before sending it to a studio."

Scene numbers. Numbered scenes are found in "production" drafts, not in new scripts being considered for purchase.

"People who include scene numbers are usually first-time writers who've picked up a production script and are using it as their model," Givens explains. "When I see scene numbers, I immediately know this is the work of a non-professional."

All of the professionals we spoke with emphasized that they'd never make a decision to buy or reject a screenplay based on presentation alone. Ultimately, the script's "quality" and the demands of the marketplace will determine whether or not it sells.

But proper formatting can increase a reader's chances of "recognizing" the quality of the work.

"The screenplay format is already choppy enough, with your eye having to move all over the place," Manetti says. "Don't add anything else that's going to be distracting and make the read any more difficult that it already is."

She likened a screenplay to a professional resume. "You want to keep it simple and slick," she says. "You wouldn't submit a resume in green neon paper, so likewise don't package your script in ways that call undue attention."

So, take the advice of industry professionals. If you want to be taken seriously, seriously observe screenwriting's "red flags." Keep it clean. Keep it simple. And eliminate any visual "clutter" that might obscure your story.

THE TEN COMMANDMENTS OF SCREENWRITING
And When to Break Them

The "rules" we apply to screenwriting were developed over time as a pragmatic way to deliver the kinds of stories audiences traditionally demand. From the plays of the ancient Greeks and Romans to the comedies and tragedies of William Shakespeare to 19th century melodramas to today's blockbuster motion pictures and TV series, the way Western Civilization chooses to tell and enjoy scripted stories has remained more or less unchanged. As Western media — particularly American (read: Hollywood) — has come to dominate our planet's culture, these "rules" of storytelling have become accepted virtually worldwide.

The great thing about movies created by screenwriting's "rules," is that they tend to produce stories with universal appeal. We all like stories with strong conflicts, with good guys worth spending time on and bad guys who ultimately get their comeuppance. We like to be told these stories in roughly ninety minutes to two and a half hours, and when the stories move us to examine our own lives or view the outside world just a little differently than we did before, we come away feeling that the experience was worthwhile.

However, like all rules, the rules of screenwriting were made to be broken. When to break the rules? There is only one acceptable answer to this question. You break the rules when the story demands it. You don't break the rules just to be "different." You don't break the rules to appear "daring." You don't break the rules to prove that you're "hip," "edgy," or "indie." You break the rules because, to do otherwise, your story could not be properly told. Period.

Here, then, are the Ten Commandments of Screenwriting...and when to break them:

1. Thou shall have a sympathetic hero.

You hear this one all the time: You have to have a hero people can root for. But some of the best "heroes" in movie history have been unapologetically unsympathetic. We like them not because they're good guys whom we want to see triumph, but because they are incredibly complex, often fatally flawed individuals who, in their often downright anti-social behavior, are just so damned *interesting*.

Some examples of well-known "unsympathetic" heroes are Ebenezer Scrooge in *A Christmas Carol*, Charles Foster Kane in *Citizen Kane*, General George S. Patton in *Patton*, Tony Montana in *Scarface*, Warren Schmidt in *About Schmidt*, and Adam Sandler in half the films he's made to date.

You can write an unsympathetic hero when you're writing a morality tale, a story about the consequences of negative behavior. In such a story, the hero is either redeemed (e.g., *A Christmas Carol*) or punished (e.g., *Scarface*), depending on the dramatic point you're trying to make. You can also write an unsympathetic hero when you're writing about the triumph of evil over good. (Hey, sometimes it happens.)

2. Thou shalt not have a weak antagonist.

Strong heroes need strong antagonists. That's what makes stories interesting. Most of the time. There are many fine films that have very weak antagonists or, in some cases, no identifiable antagonist at all (at least not of the human variety).

Some classic examples of successful films with no obvious "bad guy" are *Cast Away*, *The Big Chill*, *Four Weddings and a Funeral*, and *Groundhog Day*.

You may not need an obvious "antagonist" when you're writing a character study, a "slice-of-life" story or a biography. (Writers of true-life stories often try to fabricate or combine several actual individuals just to concoct a traditional "villain" where one did not actually exist. Most of the time, they're better off just ignoring the antagonist imperative.)

Always remember, the lack of an antagonist does not necessarily mean a lack of conflict. There can still be the conflict of man-vs-nature (*Cast Away*), man-vs-God (*Groundhog Day*), conflicting personalities (*The Big Chill*), or the best of all, man vs. woman (*Four Weddings and a Funeral*).

3. Thou shall tell thy story from a single point of view.

Many spec screenplays are criticized for having a "fractured" point of view, for failing to clearly establish who the story is about. And it's true that most of the mega-hits of the past fifty years have been stories that focused on one or perhaps two individuals.

But there are some films that intentionally shift point-of-view for dramatic effect. Perhaps the best example of this is Alfred Hitchcock's *Psycho*, which actually gives us *three* successive heroes to constantly keep the audience off-balance. Shifting point-of-view is also a great way to inject the element of surprise.

Because war is truly a group effort, many war movies take multiple points-of-view to properly portray their complex subject matter. Movies like *The Longest Day, Tora! Tora! Tora!, The Battle of Britain*, and more recently, *The Thin Red Line*, all constantly shift focus, which allows these monumental battles to be captured *in toto*.

Some movies — particularly epics — are multi-generational (e.g., *How the West Was Won, Sunshine*) and, again, must necessarily wrap up one story so as to move on to the next. They break the One-Point-of-View Commandment because there is no other way to dramatize such a massive narrative.

4. Thou shall have a clear beginning, middle, and end.

Most American movies unwind in chronological order. That's the way the universe works, and we're kind of used to it. However, there are some very effective films that succeed because they tell their stories *out* of order, either through the use of flashbacks, flash forwards, or the simple mangling of chronology.

Examples of such non-traditional screen stories include Orson Welles' *Citizen Kane* (flashbacks), Richard Lester's *Petulia* (flash forwards), Quentin Tarantino's *Pulp Fiction* (a chronological merry-go-round), Christopher Nolan's *Memento* (flashbacks combined with reverse chronology), and Charlie Kaufman's *Eternal Sunshine of the Spotless Mind* (another chronological crazy-quilt).

Feel free to mess around with your story's natural chronology whenever your themes are best revealed, when events are out of order, when your story involves simultaneous action, when your story uses a last-minute "reveal" that reframes your story, or when your movie is, in fact, about *confusion*.

5. Thou shall make thy hero American or European.

A key demand that most studios make on any film they produce is that the lead roles must be "castable," meaning they must be parts that can be played by A-List actors and actresses. In the American market, this means actors who are recognizably *American* (today, this can include African-Americans and Hispanics as well as Caucasians), or at least European, preferably British.

Although this commandment still applies to the vast majority of scripts that are and will be purchased, there are some notable exceptions (although most are recognized only in retrospect). Films like *Crouching Tiger, Hidden Dragon; The Gods Must Be Crazy, Quest for Fire*, and *The Incredible Journey* all focused on characters who were certainly not traditional American roles. In some cases, the heroes weren't even human. But the movies were produced and found audiences nonetheless.

You *can* break this rule and write non-American/European heroes when:

- Your story necessarily takes place in another time/country/culture
- You're writing young characters
- It's an action film
- It's a comedy
- It's designed to be produced on a very limited budget

In any of these situations, producers are likely to be more flexible than they would be in more traditional circumstances.

6. Thou shall have an active hero.

In the vast majority of cases, a protagonist who acts and reacts only when prompted by others — one who has no personal agenda or is simply too frightened or conflicted to do anything — is considered "weak" or "boring." Most name actors shy away from such passive roles.

However, a few passive heroes stand out as all-time classics. Forrest Gump in the movie of the same name is one of them.

Chance the gardener (aka "Chauncey Gardner") in *Being There* is another. In his delicate, episodic comedies of the 1960s, star-filmmaker Jacques Tati usually played an observer of life rather than an active participant. Oh, and that old Shakespeare guy had a pretty good passive hero, too. Name of Hamlet, I believe.

As the history of film shows, you may break this otherwise rigid commandment when:

- Your story is about the world of your hero, not the hero him/herself
- When the hero's passivity is the whole point of your story
- When your "hero" is actually a third-person narrator, á la Nick Carraway in *The Great Gatsby*

At any other time, try to keep your hero, well, heroic.

7. Thy hero shall undergo change.

Studio execs virtually *demand* change in their protagonists. Such a change is called a "character arc," and it's an imperative in the Syd Field/Robert McKee/John Truby School of Screenwriting.

The problem is, there are *lots* of films in which heroes don't change a bit. They don't learn anything. They don't reexamine themselves or their values. They don't make smarter or better choices. They just get the job done and go home.

Such heroes are often found in action films. And many of them are iconic. James Bond. Indiana Jones. Dirty Harry Callahan. These guys don't change. If they did, the franchises would die.

There's an equally large pantheon of classic "detectives" who remain constant from adventure to adventure. Sherlock Holmes. Hercule Poirot. Charlie Chan. Nary a degree of "character arc" among them.

Right up there with genres that, by nature, tend to resist character evolution are comedies. In the classic comedies of the 1930s and 1940s, "growth" in the lead comic was virtually unheard of. Charlie Chaplin, W.C. Fields, Laurel & Hardy, the Marx Brothers, Abbott and Costello, etc., may have affected change in *others*, but they always emerged from their various adventures with their characters unscathed.

Today, with virtually all filmmakers and studio folk well aware of the "rules" of screenwriting, there is far greater emphasis on character arc, even in comedies. However, every once in a while you get a *Naked Gun*, a *Dumb & Dumber*, or an *Elf* in which the hero, blithely secure in his own illusionary perfection, emerges from the story virtually unchanged.

In other words, you can have a hero who doesn't change if:
- Your hero is iconic
- Your movie is a comedy
- You're point is that *people don't change!*

8. Thy story shall have a "Wow Factor."

It's no secret that high concept has been king since the 1980s. But the idea of a "Wow Factor" — an element so original, so exciting, or so controversial that it makes audiences go, "Wow! I've got to see that film!" goes all the way back to the time when the "Wow Factor" was the fact that pictures *moved* at all.

Today, the path of least resistance still dictates that a screenplay should have at least one remarkable element in it — usually within its premise — if it's ever going to sell, get made, and be seen. However, even in recent years, there have been many critical and box office hits that have been decidedly "low concept." Just a partial list of such films would include *American Beauty*, *American Pie*, *Bridget Jones's Diary*, *In the Bedroom*, and *Rushmore*. You can probably name a half-dozen others without even breaking a sweat.

In short, this is one of the easiest commandments to get away with breaking, as long as:
- Your characters are truly interesting
- Your storyline is particularly complex
- If your jokes are *really* funny
- If you still have some exploitable elements like sex and violence

9. Thy first act shalt not occupy more than the first quarter of your screenplay.

For obsessive structuralists, this commandment is all but carved in cement in front of Grauman's Chinese Theater. Many writers — and readers — become physically unhinged whenever they find a first act that occupies more than 25 to 30 percent of a screenplay's page count. Today, movies are supposed to get moving *fast*, and to drag out a story's exposition is a one-way ticket to turnaround.

But, as with all the Commandments we've discussed, there are movies that have performed just fine with extended first acts. These include *Star Wars, City Slickers, Close Encounters of the Third Kind,* and *Full Metal Jacket,* just to name a few.

When can you have a first act that's longer than the traditional thirty pages?

- When you have a story that is likewise unusually structured (*Close Encounters of the Third Kind, Full Metal Jacket*)
- When there's so much going on that there's no sense that your story is dragging (*Star Wars*)
- It's a comedy, and the jokes are funny (*City Slickers*)

10. Thou shall have a happy ending.

Let's face it, there's a reason we have something called "The Hollywood Ending." Most people like "up" endings, and most film-makers *really* like giving people exactly what they want.

However, sometimes the nature of your story demands that things turn out differently than one might hope. In the case of a story like *Scarface,* things might turn out very, very badly indeed. However, note that an ending can still be "down" and still be very satisfying, *provided* the ending makes a valid intellectual, emotional or thematic point.

Films, both classic and recent, with "unhappy" but still totally satisfying endings include *Citizen Kane, Casablanca, Annie Hall, American Beauty, Gladiator,* and *The Manchurian Candidate.*

Feel free to break this final commandment if:

- Your hero is ennobled by death/defeat
- You need a "downer" ending to reflect your theme
- You're writing a tragedy

Rules serve a purpose. Without speed limits, there'd be chaos on the roads (and our insurance premiums would go sky high). But sometimes — for example, when a woman is in labor — it may make more sense to break the rules than to follow them. And that's when you put pedal to the metal.

When writing movies, don't worry about getting speeding tickets. Not when there's a beautiful mega-hit waiting to be born.

WRITER BEWARE
Unproduced Writers Are Tempting Prey for Hollywood's Vultures

For an unproduced or unrepresented writer, the desire to make a fast and lucrative sale can be nearly overwhelming. For those who read *Daily Variety* and *The Hollywood Reporter,* nary a week goes by without some news item about an original screenplay selling for low-to-mid-six figures. Naturally, this raises the question: *Why not me?*! Unfortunately, there are a lot of people out there eager to exploit such ambition — and that story rarely ends up well for the *exploitee.*

Although technology has changed dramatically over the last ten years, the way Hollywood does business has not. Despite the Internet and other digital breakthroughs, scripts today are sold much like they were in the 1990s, the1980s, and the 1970s: You find an accredited agent, manager, producer, or entertainment lawyer who likes your script (perhaps you do or do not have a paid option), and that person submits your script — solo or packaged — to a studio that then buys it or does not. The business hasn't changed, nor it is likely to any time soon. (For more details on this process — and how to make it work for you — read *The Hollywood Rules,* an anonymously written tome that tells the truth about Hollywood deals and how to make the best of them.)

This has not precluded wily predators from hyping the Web as a way to get your screenplay noticed, read, or even sold — for a price, of course. Some tout the "hundreds of studio executives" who subscribe to their services and offer "testimonial quotes" from customers who purportedly became rich and famous after putting their spec screenplays online. Of course, you never hear about these scripts again, nor do you ever read stories in *Premiere*, *Entertainment Weekly* or the *Los Angeles Times* about a hot new screenwriter who was discovered through one of these online services. And why don't you? *Because it doesn't happen.* Just as it has always been, Hollywood's decision-makers only have so many hours in a day and, with every decision being a potential career-breaker, they tend to pay attention only to those screenplays that come to them from trusted contacts or from agencies whose reputations are equally dependent on delivering quality product.

If you are ever tempted to subscribe to an online screenplay service that promises to blast your logline to every major player in Hollywood, here's what I want you to do first: Go down to Tijuana and go on a three-day tequila bender; when you wake up on the floor of a Mexican jail nursing a hangover the size of the State of Chihuahua, you will see things in a much clearer light and thank yourself for your prudence. Seriously, those services are that bad an idea.

(A side note about posting your ideas on the Internet. *Ideas cannot be copyrighted!* They *cannot* be legally protected! Posting even something as short as a logline on a public forum can be an invitation for theft.)

The same caveat can be offered should you encounter someone who wants to sign you to a long-term representation contract. The Writers Guild of America has very strict rules governing the agent/client relationship. One of those rules is that a signatory agent has ninety days of exclusivity — after which, if they haven't gotten you paying work, you can fire them, no questions asked. If a "representative" demands that you stay bound to him or her for a period any longer than that, then he or she is clearly not a Guild signatory, and you shouldn't have signed with him or her in the first place.

(How can you tell who and who is not a Guild signatory? Ask the WGA or check out the list on their website at www.wga.org.)

You should also stay clear of anyone who wants you to pay for representation. In the American film industry, all legitimate representatives — regardless of whether they bill themselves as agents or managers — work on a contingency basis. If they sell your script, they get a piece of the action. (By law, agents can get no more than 10 percent of your gross. Managers can charge more — generally starting at 15 percent and going as high as 30 percent.) If you don't make money, neither do they. This is what we call an "incentive." It's a system that has worked well for more than eighty years and appears sound enough to endure for another eighty more.

Avoid producers who want to tie your script up for more than ninety days without some form of remuneration. Free options are annoying, but have nonetheless become the norm over the past ten to fifteen years. You can live with a free option *if* the producer's "free ride" is of a strictly limited time. Ninety days should be plenty of time for anyone with the proper connections to get your script into the hands of viable buyers. After that, either the producer is sitting on his or her hands or your script is being shopped to second- and third-tier choices — which is not only a waste of time but also stands a good chance of "burning" your script with the industry as a whole. Stick to ninety days, after which all rights should revert back to you. And get it in writing.

Finally, if you want to employ the services of a professional screenplay analyst or company, check 'em out. Ask yourself the obvious questions: Just who *is* this guy? Does he or she have any legitimate screenwriting or studio background? How long has he or she been in business? Have the analyst's suggestions ever resulted in a script that's been sold, let alone actually been produced? Ask for references. A legitimate analyst should have no trouble providing you with dozens. And keep one hand firmly on your wallet. Although some "analysts" charge as much as $4,000 a pop, a good in-depth review and set of page notes should only cost you a tenth of that. Don't be fooled by lines like, "You get what you pay for." If that was true, admission to most summer "blockbusters" would be $1.75.

Surviving the Hollywood jungle is a challenge for even the most skilled and experienced players. The industry is fraught with traps just waiting to ensnare the naïve or blindly ambitious. But just as "You can't cheat an honest man," you *can* avoid becoming another grease slick on Hollywood Boulevard by understanding that there are no shortcuts, no instant roads to fame and fortune. To win the Hollywood game you have to play the Hollywood game — by the same rules that govern everyone else.

The good news is, it's done every day. There are plenty of opportunities for you to make your mark. Just don't become one.

Hollywood Pitch Festival™

A unique opportunity to present your story ideas to over 140 film and television buyers. Meet one-on-one and pitch your ideas in real pitch meetings. The largest festival of its kind! *August*

from CONCEPT to SALE
Conference & Pitchfest

Scott Frank & Frank Darabont

SUBMIT YOUR PROJECT TO AGENTS & MANAGERS
ATTEND CLASS SESSIONS WITH OSCAR-NOMINATED FILMMAKERS
NETWORK AT CATERED RECEPTION *February*

PowerPitch Fest™
11th Annual Hollywood Screenwriters Conference™

.: Agency Submissions
.: Vital Industry Contacts
.: Pitch Classes by A-list Filmmakers

OVER 70 EXECUTIVES, AGENTS, MANAGERS AND PRODUCERS (INCLUDING WARNER BROS., PARAMOUNT, WILLIAM MORRIS AGENCY, DREAMWORKS, HBO, MIRAMAX FILMS, ENDEAVOR AND MORE) TO MEET WITH/PITCH YOUR PROJECT TO IN ONE-ON-ONE 7-MINUTE MEETINGS. *May & October*

Master Class
an advanced course in screenwriting

You've read all the books. Listened to all the self proclaimed "gurus." Attended all the seminars. Now it's time to really learn what it takes to become a "working" Hollywood writer.

"Those two days exceeded my expectations. I've benefited significantly from the experience [and] feel like I've been on creative steroids ever since. I can't stress enough how much I've profited from this class, almost on a daily basis. Being able to tell an engaging, entertaining story has always enthralled me. Understanding how to realistically go about becoming a professional screenplay writer has been my priority for several years now. Over the course of that weekend, I felt the uncertain path before me cleared considerably. I will always feel indebted to you."

- Brad Kinney

David Benioff, Screenwriter (*Troy*)
Fade In Enthusiast

FADE IN
THE FIRST WORD IN FILM
www.fadeinonline.com

FOR THE SCREENWRITER

FINAL DRAFT PRESENTS **ASK THE PROS: SCREENWRITING**
101 Questions Answered by Industry Professionals
Edited by Howard Meibach and Paul Duran

Can't sell your screenplay? Problems with your third act? No relatives in the "biz"? Then ask the pros! Final Draft screenwriting software has secured the services of top studio and television executives, literary agents, managers, script consultants, producers and produced screenwriters to answer the most important questions on the minds of developing and emerging screenwriters. Professionals from ICM, UTA, Writers & Artists Group International, DreamWorks, Paramount, and many more take the time to stop and answer your questions. Our experts will tell the reader what's right and what's wrong with a screenplay and how to fix it. They're tough and will tell you what you *need* to hear rather than what you want to hear.
$17.95, ISBN 1-58065-056-2

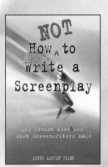

HOW NOT TO WRITE A SCREENPLAY
101 Common Mistakes Most Screenwriters Make
by Denny Martin Flinn

Having read tons of screenplays as an executive, Denny Martin Flinn has come to understand that while all good screenplays are unique, all bad screenplays are the same. Flinn's book will teach the reader how to avoid the pitfalls of bad screenwriting, and arrive at one's own destination intact. Every example used is gleaned from a legitimate screenplay. Flinn's advice is a no-nonsense analysis of the latest techniques for crafting first-rate screenplays that sell.
$16.95, ISBN 1580650155

THE SCREENPLAY WORKBOOK:
The Writing Before the Writing
by Jeremy Robinson and Tom Mungovan

Every time a screenwriter sits down to write a screenplay, he has to grapple with the daunting question of, "Where do I start?" The preparation time, or the writing *before* the writing, can be intimidating. *The Screenplay Workbook* is an instructional manual combined with proprietary worksheets, charts and fill-in lists designed to give screenwriters a better way to focus on the task of writing a screenplay. All of the organization is done, the right questions are asked, the important subjects are covered.
$18.95, ISBN 1580650538

FROM SCRIPT TO SCREEN
The Collaborative Art of Filmmaking, 2nd Edition
by Linda Seger and Edward J. Whetmore

Join Dr. Linda Seger and Edward Whetmore as they examine recent screenplays on their perilous journey from script to screen. In addition to completely updating and revising the first edition, the authors have added a substantial new section that is an extensive case study of the Academy Award® winning film, *A Beautiful Mind*, including exclusive participation by Ron Howard. In interviews with over 70 of the top professionals in the film industry, Seger and Whetmore examine each artist's role in making a great script into a great film.
$18.95, ISBN 1580650546

FOR THE SCREENWRITER

POWER SCREENWRITING
The 12 Stages of Story Development
by Michael Chase Walker

Michael Chase Walker offers a clear and straightforward framework upon which to build story plots. Standing on the broad shoulders of Joseph Campbell, Christopher Vogler, and others who have demonstrated how mythology is used, Walker brings passion, insight and clarity to a whole new range of story traditions never before examined. Walker offers a wide variety of alternative principles and techniques that are more flexible, adaptable and relevant for the modern storyteller. This book gives insight into the art of storytelling as a way to give depth and texture to any screenplay.
$19.95, ISBN 1580650414

THE COMPLETE WRITER'S GUIDE TO HEROES & HEROINES
Sixteen Master Archetypes
by Tami D. Cowden, Caro LaFever, Sue Viders

By following the guidelines of the archetypes presented in this comprehensive reference work, writers can create extraordinarily memorable characters and elevate their writing to a higher level. The authors give examples of well-known heroes and heroines from television and film so the reader can picture the archetype in his or her mind. The core archetype tells the writer how heroes or heroines think and feel, what drives them and how they reach their goals.
$17.95, ISBN 1580650244

WRITING SHORT FILMS
Structure and Content for Screenwriters
by Linda J. Cowgill

Contrasting and comparing the differences and similarities between feature films and short films, screenwriting professor Linda Cowgill offers readers the essential tools necessary to make their writing crisp, sharp and compelling. Emphasizing characters, structure, dialogue and story, Cowgill dispels the "magic formula" concept that screenplays can be constructed by anyone with a word processor and a script formatting program.
$19.95, ISBN 0943728800

SECRETS OF SCREENPLAY STRUCTURE
How to Recognize and Emulate the Structural Frameworks of Great Films
by Linda J. Cowgill

Linda Cowgill articulates the concepts of successful screenplay structure in a clear language, based on the study and analysis of great films from the thirties to present day. *Secrets of Screenplay Structure* helps writers understand how and why great films work, and how great form and function can combine to bring a story alive.
$16.95, ISBN 158065004X

FOR THE FILMMAKER

THE DIGITAL VIDEO FILMMAKER'S HANDBOOK, 2nd Edition
by Maxie D. Collier

Maxie Collier's book covers the creative and technical aspects of digital shooting and is designed to provide detailed, practical information on DV filmmaking. Collier delves into the mechanics and craft of creating personal films and introduces the reader to the essential terminology, concepts, equipment and services required to produce a quality DV feature film. Includes DVD.
$26.95, ISBN 1580650589

THE INDIE PRODUCER'S HANDBOOK
Creative Producing from A to Z
by Myrl A. Schreibman

Myrl Schreibman has written a straightforward, insightful and articulate account of what it takes to make a successful feature film. Filled with engaging and useful anecdotes, Schreibman provides a superlative introduction and overview to all the key elements of producing feature films. Useful to film students and filmmakers as a theoretical and practical guide to understanding the filmmaking process.
$21.95, ISBN 1580650376

FILM PRODUCTION
The Complete *UNCENSORED* Guide to Independent Filmmaking
by Greg Merritt

Merritt cuts through the fluff and provides the reader with real-world facts about producing and selling a low-budget motion picture. Topics covered include: pre-production, principal photography, post-production, distribution, script structure and dialogue, raising money, limited partnerships, scheduling and budgeting, cast and crew, production equipment, scoring, publicity, festivals, foreign distribution, video and more.
$24.95, ISBN 0943728991

THE ULTIMATE FILM FESTIVAL SURVIVAL GUIDE, 3rd Edition
by Chris Gore

Learn the secrets of successfully marketing and selling your film at over 600 film festivals worldwide. Author Chris Gore reveals how to get a film accepted and what to do after acceptance, from putting together a press kit to putting on a great party to actually closing a deal. Gore includes an expanded directory section, new interviews as well as a new chapter that details a case study of the most successful independent film to date, *The Blair Witch Project*.
$21.95, ISBN 1580650570

HOLLYWOOD CREATIVE DIRECTORY

HOLLYWOOD CREATIVE DIRECTORY, 52nd Edition

Single issue $64.95
1-year subscription $164.95
2-year subscription $279.95

- Studios and Networks
- Film and TV Executives
- Production Companies
- Independent Producers
- TV Shows and Staff
- Projects in Development
- Production Tracking
- Selected Credits

HOLLYWOOD REPRESENTATION DIRECTORY, 28th Edition

Single issue $64.95
1-year subscription $109.95
2-year subscription $189.95

- Talent & Literary Agents
- Personal Managers
- Entertainment Attorneys
- Business Affairs Departments
- Publicity Companies
- Casting Directors

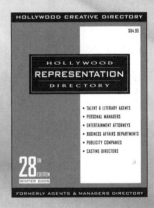

2004 BLU-BOOK PRODUCTION DIRECTORY

Single issue...$74.95

The Hollywood Creative Directory in association with The Hollywood Reporter is proud to present the *2004 Blu-Book Production Directory*—containing more than 200 product and service categories with thousands of listings. The directory is organized into 10 major tabbed sections that represent all the services and personnel necessary to take a film, TV, commercial or music video project from concept to completion. The *Blu-Book* also includes below-the-line craft professionals with credit and contact information. From camera rentals to sound stages to costumes to special effects to props to finding an animal for a production, it can all be found in this directory—truly "the Yellow Pages of Hollywood." Now includes expanded New York production listings.

ABOUT THE AUTHOR

Allen B. Ury has been a professional writer for more than twenty-five years, with a career that spans such fields as advertising, public relations and communications marketing as well as professional screen and television writing. He has more than fifteen juvenile fiction and non-fiction books to his credit as well as scores of magazine articles.

As a screenwriter, he has sold projects to Walt Disney Studios, New Line Cinema, Fries Entertainment, Weintraub/Kuhn Productions, Concorde, Wizan Films, and many others. He joined the Writers Guild of America-West in 1989.

Since 1993, Allen has served as Senior Screenplay Analyst for *Fade In* and has contributed notes and analysis to more than 3,000 screenplays. He has been a staff writer for *Fade In* magazine since 1995 and pens its regular "Master Class" column. He frequently lectures on screenwriting at various industry events.

Allen currently resides in Orange County with his wife, Rene, son Robert and "Doc" the dachshund. If you'd like to contact Allen directly, please feel free to email him at allen@fadeinonline.com